Who Says The Poor Must Stay Poor?

Who Says The Poor Must Stay Poor?

'A Strategy moving you from third world to first world productivity'

Dr. James Okpanachi

 www.trafford.com

North America & international
toll-free: 844-688-6899 (USA & Canada)
fax: 812 355 4082

Contents

DEDICATION

This book is dedicated to my late sister Comfort Okpanachi, a God-given strength and support.

ACKNOWLEDGEMENT

This book, being a product of the "Mastermind" principle, leaves me indebted to many great minds who instructed and inspired me over the years providing the foundation for me to write this book.

To my natural cover, Air Cdre Okpanachi (rtd), Chief Mrs Okpanachi, Mrs Margaret Chukwudi. The atmosphere of love you always provided was just right for my growth and development.

To my spiritual cover: Rev George Adegboye and Pastor Matthew Ashimolowo I say a big thank you.

A big hand to all my angels who are too numerous to mention.

Evelyn Okpanachi, my helpmate and my little girls Shekinah and Neriah; thanks for all the love and support.

INTRODUCTION

Coming To Terms With The Terms

Having had the privilege of travelling to several countries outside Africa, I find myself weeping many times as I long to see the unfurling of productivity and prosperity in the part of the world I come from and mankind in general. The state of Africa, Third World people and the untapped potential in the world have always been a puzzle to me, as I wonder how nation states so blessed with people and resources could be left so unharnessed. This burden has led to the writing of this book which serves as the logical presentation of the vision of the ROYAL INITIATIVE AGAINST POVERTY: RAISING A PEOPLE WITHOUT POVERTY.

This inquiry has led me to study the history of several rich industrialised nations. I have equally read through the works of great minds with a similar passion.

Your definition will determine your direction and your direction will determine your destination

I have had many sleepless nights thinking, pondering and praying for answers to this paradox. This book is the product of my efforts to get to the root of this predicament.

It will help the UN to achieve its goal of global equalisation. It will also help the world body to achieve to a great extent the eight Millennium Development Goals by 2020.

I intend to partner with the African Union, and core stakeholders in the fight against underdevelopment in the continent. It will help individuals unlock their wealth from within. This book has what it takes to spark a Third World revolution. It is a practical well thought out set of ideas that will show you the way out of Poverty into Productivity.

It is not a hidden fact that many individuals and countries with a lot of potential are still down the productivity and prosperity line. This is because potential is not enough. It has to be mixed with certain ingredients to produce true and lasting wealth. We will explore how individuals, organisations and countries must get out of Third World situations of underdevelopment and get rooted in first world possibilities. This book will identify our true enemy; and will also go a step further to unveil information that will help to neutralise it.

You cannot be influential without the presence of potential

The quest for a better life and the force of need has resulted in many discoveries and inventions; and an accumulation of lots of profound knowledge. The knowledge so described is simply any information which when combined with application could lead to a positive improvement in the quality of life we live. I believe what you are about to read will serve as PROFOUND KNOWLEDGE for your country, organisation, family and for you as a person. It will help you unlock the resource of wealth within you.

The principles presented in this book have universal application and can be customised for any Third World country or Third World person, or anyone desiring to increase in his/her level of productivity and performance.

I believe your desire for change has brought you to this book and change you will get. Tighten your belt as you come along with me into a wealth of knowledge that will change your material and spiritual condition and inevitably your immediate environment. Get ready for a revolution.

One of the problems I have discovered in the world today is lack of understanding. We develop and act in the wrong direction because we have defined concepts and words wrongly. A definition is what forms your mental configuration and your mental configuration affects your perception in life. Our concept of power, prosperity, productivity, wealth, happiness and success is often off target. This is rooted in the definitions in our minds.

If a man defines success as having a car and a house, the moment he achieves this goal, it becomes his success destination and at this *Where there is no proper definition there will be deviation* point he becomes closed and unconsciously passive to progress. If you define power as being in a political position, you will do anything; even break all rules of life to achieve political power. Many have defined wealth as having chains of cars, so they pursue things rather than purpose. Your definition will determine your direction; your direction will determine your destination.

We must re-define and re-programme our minds so we can act right. Certain viruses have infected our mental software so our programs are not functioning as well as they should. I am about to edit, or better still delete, such wrong concepts. Some stereotypes etched on your mental monitors have to be erased for the expansion of your possibilities.

The right information, which is what you are about to receive, will put you in proper position to get to your destiny.

When you define wealth as the amount of lives you have touched, your life will gravitate towards touching lives. When you define leadership as a function and not a position, you will be relevant. Wherever you find yourself, you will always be a blessing and not a liability to humanity. If you will rightly define words you will see things refined on your behalf.

A Nation or A Country

The understanding of these two words will help governments, organisations and families to give proper leadership that will lead to true development and productivity in our specific environments. A nation is that which makes a country what it is; it gives a country its wholeness and productivity. One error Third World countries have made is to focus on "the country" and not "the nation". A nation is like the skeletal system of a person, which is not too visible, but is that

Let us build our people and our people will build our cities

which gives shape and structure to that entity. It is the root behind the fruit.

A nation is a people; a country is a place or geographical location. We tend in the Third World countries, to immediately want our countries to look like America, England, France and other developed countries resulting in huge investments in buildings, infrastructures and areas that just beautify the environments giving a false sense of satisfaction, but the lives of the people are not touched by our leadership. I intend to help governments, organisations and people rightly prioritise their pattern of leadership, as more investments should be made in people rather than in an aesthetic environment. I love the motto of LEGACEE, it simply says: *knowledge grows our people and our people grow our organisation.* Any growth or change that does not begin with people will only be an illusion and can never be real and lasting. Let us build our people and our people will build our cities.

Third World Countries, Third World People

The term Third World generally refers to underdevelopment; it refers to a standard of living that is below the human development index set by the United Nations. Third World countries are places where the average human development index is below average. A Third World country is said to be one in which a larger percentage of the people live below the poverty line, that is, less than one dollar per day, this also goes for a Third World person.

A Third World person, is not someone from a Third World country; it is a person that has not developed his/her capacity for productivity

Milder words are being used to describe underdeveloped countries. The fact still remains that certain people and countries are not developed to their capacity. I will be using this term for the purpose of illustration.

I wish to say however that being Third World really has nothing to do with where you are from or the colour of your skin, but the level of your personal development. It has to do with how much you have developed your capacity for productivity. There are many people who hail from Third World countries who by their level of productivity are first world people and vice versa. You could even have a lot of money and yet be a Third World person. If someone steals money from the government or is involved in fraudulent deals, he has broken the principled lifestyle of a first world person. I believe it is a status that can only be attributed to men of character and productivity.

I will be emphasising productivity above prosperity. Human development which will always have a ripple effect on community development as first world people will always produce first world countries. No matter your level, as you read this book, it is bound to enhance your development which will help you to become prominent. I want to say to every Third World country, as you begin to get involved in developing your people into first class citizens, they will automatically begin to act in ways that will lead to developing the environment. Someone once said that *places derive value from people and not people from places*. It is true that some environments assist performance but traveling to these places does not solve the problem automatically. It is possible to be productive wherever you are if you are ready to go through the pain and process of development. Develop your spirit, develop your mind, develop your body and experience the transformation of your life to another level.

Poverty, Productivity and Prosperity

The conventional definition of poverty is the lack of money. This concept of poverty is usually divided into three;

1) Extreme poverty refers to individuals who survive on less than one dollar per day, it also refers to countries in which seventy five percent of the entire population survive on less than one dollar per day.

2) Moderate poverty refers to a situation in which an individual survives on less than two dollars per day.

> *Poverty is not the lack of money, it is the lack of ability to make money*

3) Relative poverty refers to individuals who cannot afford to have a social status (entertainment, sports, etc.).

Recently, there has been an emergence of a group described as 'core poor' who live on less than fifty pence a day.

However I would like to redirect our attention in this book from money to ability; my definition of poverty is not the absence of money but the lack of ability for productivity. I will be emphasising personal productivity as the way out of poverty. Every man has an inherent ability built into him by God. If this ability is discovered, developed and directed there are no limits to what he can attain.

Get ready for this adventure, it will reveal your identity, it will activate your ability, it will enhance your productivity, it will challenge your creativity and it will establish your prosperity. What you are about to read can revolutionise any man, any family, any organisation and any country. Dr Nelson Mandela once said "Africa is beyond bemoaning the past for its problems. The task of undoing the past is on the shoulders of African leaders themselves, with the support of those . . . who know that Africa must take responsibility for its own destiny, that Africa will uplift itself only by its own methods in partnership with those who wish her well." Jump onto this bandwagon of change, it is not about a person, it is about a people, a people who are tired of the status quo, a people who know things can and will be better. This revolution will not be complete without you, get sparked up, don't stay closed; don't stay shut, get into the mood and buzz of things and contribute your quota and play your part.

Why should people blessed with potential remain in abject poverty? Countries that do not have as much natural resources as most African countries are much more productive. Independence has not truly made us free; we are still slaves to corruption, violence, lack of productivity and extreme poverty. There is a missing link between potential, productivity and prosperity. It is this link that I intend to provide. I will present a technology that will work for any one that will rightly apply it. Every question has an answer, every puzzle a solution, every storm an end. Time for true change has come,

Personal development must take place before organisational and national development

that is why you are reading this book. Africa is in poverty because the majority of Africans are poor. It must first start with the individual before the collective mass of people. I will provide enough information to provide movement up the ladder of prosperity. What you are about to read will give you the push and the momentum to press through the barricades of limitations, to the other side of the mountain. This is the answer to the question, the solution to the puzzle you have been working on. Get ready for true and lasting prosperity.

I am not insinuating however that this book contains all the answers. It is volume one in a series of seven; it is a work in partnership with the thoughts and efforts of many great minds to put an end once and for all to extreme hunger and poverty in people, Africa and other Third World countries. Dr Nelson Mandela also said "overcoming poverty is not a gesture of charity. It is an act of justice. It is the protection of a fundamental human right, the right to dignity and a decent life." It was in this same spirit that Martin Luther King Jnr said, "Our lives begin to end the day we become silent about things that matter." That is why I have refused to remain quiet. You must join the many voices and forces either by speaking or acting. Begin to take steps towards

Productivity is the way out of poverty into prosperity

a life of productivity and prosperity, your progress is the progress of the world.

PART ONE

THE PARADOX AND THE PEOPLE

'There are Laws that erase Flaws'

CHAPTER ONE:

UNVEILING THE ENEMY

In every man there is the innate desire for productivity and prosperity. This probably explains why we abhor being poor. It is for this same reason that there is a movement of people from poorer to richer countries. Man always wants to dwell in an environment of prosperity. If you have the desire for prosperity, I am glad to tell you, you are in the right boat. It will only enhance your capacity to be of use to your world. Productivity and prosperity are vital ingredients that are of paramount importance for any man and country to fulfill its destiny. To live in poverty is to live a life alien to mankind. The existence of this monster today does not make it right. Poverty is a monster that must be fought and defeated. To fold our hands and wish things would change and situations improve is simply a mirage. It is a primitive level of insanity to think that things will just get better by doing nothing. Certain critical buttons must be pressed, certain laws that make men lords must be applied; nothing just happens, things are made to happen.

Every battle requires strategy, intensity, artillery and accuracy to end up in victory

This book is part of my contribution to the global fight to eradicate poverty from our lives and countries. You are bound to find jewels at every point, enough to power your life to the next level. You are bound to discover what it takes to create the kind of environment you want, it does not take struggles, it takes steps.

In my opinion, approaching life as a battle is one of the best ways to relate to life. The Herculean task of going into military battle provides enough information which if applied will bring one face to face with victory against poverty. Every battle requires a level of strategy, intensity, capacity, accuracy and artillery. To be placid and complacent in the face of the mounting challenges of life is to invite defeat. The wealth of knowledge you will glean will provide this intensity and sharpen your accuracy; it will give you some fire power and help you to develop a strategy as you battle poverty in your life and environment.

In order to address this problem of poverty, the United Nations Millennium Declaration was adopted in September 2000, at the largest gathering of heads of governments. This gathering charged nations, both rich and poor to do all they can to eradicate poverty, promote human dignity and equality. The goals include those dedicated to:

1) Eradicate extreme poverty and hunger
2) Achieve universal primary education
3) Promote gender equality and empower women
4) Reduce child mortality
5) Improve maternal health
6) Combat HIV/AIDS, malaria and other disease
7) Ensure environmental sustainability
8) Develop a global partnership for development

Poverty eradication has remained the issue for individuals, organisations, families and countries. It has remained the core issue in African governments. For instance in Nigeria, a medium term development programme; The National Economic Empowerment and Development Strategy (NEEDS), is directed at poverty reduction, which is meant to benefit all segments of the Nigerian society, especially women and other unalienable groups. The main strategy, of this programme includes technology and skill acquisition, natural resource management, infrastructure(physical and social) development, non-farm activities and human capital development. In addition, the area of agro-industrial development is meant to reduce rural poverty as is partnership between the public and private sectors.

Shedding Light on the Fight

The fight against poverty cannot be left to international financial institutions, wealthy and industrialised countries or even governments. It is a fight that requires a committed and concerted effort to floor this monster. There are three dimensions of warfare that we must understand as we battle this monster so that we don't end up throwing punches in the air.

Life is not all about funfair, it's about warfare

1) Blind warfare
2) Shadow warfare
3) Target warfare

Blind warfare refers to going to battle when the enemy has not yet been identified. I think poverty has remained prevalent, because certain root causes and salient issues have not yet been addressed. One of the things I will be doing is unveiling core issues; where the rubber hits the road. I will narrow this battle as realistically as possible, highlighting where to hit the enemy to achieve the result of prosperity. The enemy you cannot identify, you cannot nullify. Enough of struggling: get ready to take calculated steps to your prosperity.

Shadow warfare refers to battling poverty where the enemy has been identified, but one is distracted from the salient issues due to factors such as irresponsibility, laziness, corruption and greed etc. Hitting shadows will never get the monster of poverty down. Weak men talk of chances but strong men talk of cause and effect. I will be drawing your attention to the real issues so you can score the bull's eye.

The quality of your light, will determine the quality of your life

Target warfare entails fighting an identified enemy. It refers to directing your energy where it matters; dealing with all majors and not minors. It involves concentration of power. It is this kind of warfare that can bring down the monster of poverty. It will save energy and time. It will require technology, it will require skill.

Switching on the Light

Poverty is not as mysterious as many have made it out to be. It is life and labour in the midst of darkness that makes one grope and struggle, ending up with bruises. In the Hebrew 15 context, information is likened to light while darkness is likened to ignorance. Anytime you get informed, you see clearly and better, you understand the reason for things, you know what to do and where to go, you are acquainted with which buttons to press to make things work. In the midst of information (light) you are not guessing, you can act with a level of accuracy; hitting this monster right on target with an anticipated positive result.

The reason for much damage today, is little knowledge

Anytime you go into battle without relevant and current information (light), you fight in the midst of darkness (ignorance). The quality of your light will affect the quality of your life. In any situation in which darkness threatens, go for light. We must become readers in search of knowledge and wisdom. We must possess the hunter's instincts in respect to information, it will take the sweat out, it will energize and drive your person, and it will increase your probability for victory against poverty. In other words, anywhere poverty thrives it is because ignorance prevails. To switch on the information bulb is actually the first step to fighting poverty. It is interesting to know that the Hebrew concept for light also symbolizes productivity and prosperity while darkness symbolizes poverty. Have you ever switched on the light bulb and darkness refused to vanish? If it remained, probably something was wrong with the electrical system. Darkness "always" responds to light, it does not argue or struggle. There is a better way to fight; it is fighting in the midst of light. Our societies today are knowledge driven. You and your organisation cannot live isolated from the global community. Begin to change your life and your country by 16 acquiring the relevant information it takes to effect a positive change. If people would only follow financial intelligence half as much as they follow finance itself, most of their money problems would be solved.

I remember staying with an instructor of mine by the name of Ohi for a couple of months. His understanding of the financial industry was so amazing. I remember going from bank to bank with him getting first hand practical information about the banking industry. It felt as though a whole new world of opportunities had just opened for me. I was always amazed by certain people spending billions buying companies, opening new businesses and so on. I never knew a lot of these billionaires had certain working relationships with financial institutions. I learnt concepts such as counterpart funding.

The poverty problem, is actually a productivity problem

This same period I learnt about corporate social responsibility. I wasn't aware that certain companies by law were supposed to support ideas that were geared towards human and community development. I always thought this kind of partnership existed with the entertainment industry since it was popular and financially lucrative. I was quite naïve, wasn't I? But it's a different story today. You too can begin your journey on the path of discovery, and recover all you have ever lost. You will be surprised how a little piece of information can radically change your life for the better. Many discoveries I have made have helped put me where I am today. The school of learning is one school you cannot afford to ever graduate from. Discover something new today that will give you a competitive advantage in your area of operation. Search for knowledge, search for truth. That person you admire knows something you don't; the moment you make your discoveries you will be ready for your flight.

The word poverty is a dominant theme, as it is the reason for this book. It is the absence of productivity and not the absence of money. Productivity will always bring prosperity. The question is how productive are you? How much in terms of goods and services come out of you to better someone else either directly or indirectly? Productive people, organisations and countries are actually prosperous always. The poverty problem is really just a productivity problem. In a nutshell, to become productive is to become prosperous. I challenge you to begin to work at harnessing your potential, to challenge your creativity to a point where you become relevant to yourself and your country.

The difference between a first and a Third World person is not the colour of skin but the colour of mind

Poverty is manifested in many ways, ranging from the visible to the invisible. The tangible orvisible are underlined by the lack of money, the lack of access to basic services and investment capital, an escalating number of resource based conflicts, increased child labour, unemployment, high crime rates, high mortality rates, low literacy, brain drain, growing urban slums, breakdown of society safety nets, rural urban drifts, prevalence of the HIV/AIDS pandemic etc. The invisible characteristics of poverty encapsulate the underlying causes of poverty: Poor self esteem, lack of motivation, discouragement. It is also underscored by the broader national and international actions or inactions on governance and accountability that reinforce and sustain poverty. In our fight against poverty it is right to give proper definitions, as this will boost clarification so we can all work towards its eradication.

A Lesson for Third World People

A little boy went with his father to visit an uncle during the summer holidays. This uncle was a very successful livestock farmer. The farm extended over several acres of land. All kinds of animals were bred on this expansive farmland; cows, goats, fish, pigs and horses. The little boy had never seen so many animals in one place in his life. Every morning, he would wake up with excitement to behold God's wonderful creatures. He noticed something very peculiar about the pigs. He wondered why they would always play in the mud. No matter how much the farm hands tried to clean them up in the night they were dirty by morning. He decided to separate one of the young pigs from the other dirty ones to take care of it specially. He

Any change without, that is not rooted within, cannot be true and lasting

created a very clean environment for it to live in; he made sure all the feeding and bathing equipment were all sterilised, ready to change the lifestyle of his new pet. As soon as the sun gave its first sign of waking up from sleep, at the first crow of the cock, the little boy jumped up from bed and ran swiftly down the stairs literally floating through the house. He was about to get the shock of his life. The little clean pig had dug into the ground and was playing in the mud which it had created and seemed to enjoy the puddle very much.

As a National Reformer with an African origin, I have met with different kinds of people. I have seen Africans who are first world people and vice versa. The reason is not farfetched. It is one of the reasons the fight against poverty seems like a Herculean task. We have disobeyed the law of sequencing, we have majored on the minor and minored on the majors; a problem of priority. Some things cannot happen until other things happen. Just like our farm story, the little boy did not know that the internal configurations of pigs are tailored in such a way that their habitat has to be around dirt. Bathing the pigs, creating a clean and new environment was not the issue. All outward activity that does not change the mental configuration cannot be long-lasting.

No one, no country, deserves to live in poverty. We all must have a decent shot at prosperity, but it must begin from within. It must start with the state of mind. We must begin to think productivity and prosperously. This thinking pattern will lead to certain behavioural patterns

Every thinking mind, leads to a rising life

that will change the circumstances of our lives and countries. If we want to change, we must first change our thinking. The difference between a first and a Third World person is the state of their mind not the place they are from. The state of your mind actually determines the state of your life. Receiving information is not sufficient. We must allow what we hear and read to positively tinker with our thinking patterns. There are certain actions that always lead to production, there is a lifestyle of the rich; smart work, hard work, planning, saving, investing, time management. But all this is rooted in a state of mind.

Do you know that at least eight million people die every year because they are too poor to live? Many people are underdeveloped mentally. This explains why underdeveloped countries still exist. You should stop misdirecting your time, energy and resources. Your mind can actually power your life. It is like the engine of a car, which is not seen but is the actual force behind motion and progress of the vehicle. Start thinking in line with production, impact and influence. What can I do to better my environment? How can I improve the status of those around me? Start thinking of a life beyond yourself. This is the pattern of greatness. Start thinking technology, start thinking industry. Begin to think right, act right and things will inevitably become right.

Facing Facts

- An average of two million children will die this year because the world governments have failed to reduce poverty levels.
- According to UNICEF 30,000 children die daily due to poverty.
- 8 million people die yearly because they are too poor to live.
- A few hundred millionaires now own as much as the world's poorest 2.5 billion people.
- The combined wealth of the world's 2000 richest people was $1 trillion in 1999, the combined income of the 582 million people living in the 43 least developed countries then was $146 billion.
- The Gross Domestic Product (GDP) of the poorest 48 countries (i.e. 25% of the world's countries), is less than the wealth of the world's 3 richest people combined.
- The world's 497 billionaires in 2001 registered a combined wealth of $1.54 trillion, well over the combined gross national products of all countries of the Sub Saharan Africa ($929 billion).

- In 1960, 20% of the world's people in the richest countries had 30 times the income of the poorest 20%, in 1997, 74 times as much.
- An analysis of long term trends shows the difference between the richest and the poorest countries was about:
- 3 to 1 in 1820
- 11 to 1 in 1913
- 35 to 1 in 1950
- 44 to 1 in 1973
- 72 to 1 in 1992

These statistics are self explanatory and can wake up any sleeping giant. While some people have elected to stay stagnant; humans like you are taking giant strides towards achieving their destiny. Men have become as large as countries, single countries have become as large as many put together. It is important to know that these individuals and countries all have their own stories to tell. If others have done it, you can begin to accept the challenge, accept the needed responsibility to be better and bigger by helping others climb as you climb up the ladder of success.

Your development will enhance your capacity to be prominent

What Others Are Saying

- Pope John Paul (II) spoke of the unjust social structures as "the structures of sin" for they are the products of human actions and make it difficult to change a poor person's situation. These sinful structures which are the ultimate causes of poverty are largely produced by the desire for excessive wealth, control and status. For example in Africa one does not need to look beyond our national borders to realise that while the majority of the African population moves more deeply into poverty, a distinct minority is accumulating wealth.

- Tony Blair, former Prime Minister of Great Britain said that removing poverty in Africa remains the fundamental challenge of our generation. Africa can change and become better. He told the World Economic Forum in Davors, Switzerland that the African poverty is a "scar on the conscience of the world".

- Bono, the famous rock star said: "There is a continent Africa being armed by flames, when the history books are written, our age will be remembered by three things, the war on terror, the digital revolution and what we did or did not do to put the fire out of Africa".

- George Warner, an educationalist, says poverty in Africa is a reality that is a struggle, one day at a time; poverty has brought some to a lessening of their humanity, and it is as much about powerlessness and exclaiming as about low levels of wealth and income. It is as much a social, cultural, political and religious reality as it is an economic one.

It is a clear fact that Africa, Third World countries and many individuals are not what they should be. As we climb the ladder of productivity and prosperity, tighten your seat belts, be active all the way. I believe by the time you are through with this book, your desire and drive for a better life and a better country will have been ignited.

CHAPTER TWO:

PARADIGMS AND PROSPERITY

I first heard the word "paradox" in Senior School. My very interesting literature teacher used to use illustrations such as "water water everywhere not any drop to drink" to put across his points. It worked because that impression has not left me since then. Little productivity in the midst of much potential. Poverty in the midst of plenty seems to be the description of Third World countries and Third World people.

The way out of the paradox, is connecting, challenging and channelling potential to productivity.

Potential is that which is, but has not yet been; that which can be used but has not yet been used. I categorically say that the way out of this paradox is connecting, challenging and channeling unharnessed potential to yield productivity.

The Paradox (A case study of Nigeria)

Nigeria is an enormously rich country with a large expanse of land. Since the discovery of oil, Nigeria has earned over \$320 billion from crude oil in more than three decades. This is in addition to other resource flows such as loans and aids. Despite this enormous wealth, the trend of poverty between 1980 and 1996 as reported by the Federal Office of Statistics (FOS) within three broad categories: The non-poor, moderate poor and core poor depict that that the number of core poor has risen by 6.2% in 1980 to 29.3% in 1996. In the same period, the total percentage below the poverty line has risen from 28.1% in 1990 to 65.6% in 1996. The *Learning from history can* total population considered to *help secure your destiny* be poor rose correspondingly from 17.7% in 1980 to 61.1% in 1996. Incidence of poverty in 2000/2001 is estimated as 70%, indicating that over 80 million people are living below the poverty line. From the *indicative percentage of the incidence of poverty in Nigeria*, it is said that two out of every three Nigerians are poor.

Literature on the causes of poverty in Nigeria affirms that Nigeria is one of the poorest countries in the world, *measured mainly by the degree of income inequality*. Despite her abundant natural resources and ranking as the eighth exporter of oil, Nigeria ranks about the worst in sub—Saharan Africa in social statistics. According to the World Bank, the poor in Nigeria have a cash income that is insufficient to cover minimum standards of food, fuel, shelter, medical care and schooling. In the human development report (2000), Nigeria ranked among the 20 poorest countries in the world. The UNDP states that, "Nigeria is one of the poorest countries in the world . . . She is worse off today than she was in the 1980s". If we are truly the giant of Africa, we are either hallucinating or this so called giant has gone to sleep. (This statistic is similar with respect to other Third World countries.)

However, one of the goals this book intends is to change our focus from external to internal. If aid given to Third World countries is only financial, we will forever remain slaves to the first world countries even if the capital investments are used for roads, hospitals and for the provision of other basic amenities. We need to be mentally empowered to be truly free people. We don't just need the money; we need the mind that makes the money. In my opinion, poverty is beyond the lack of money; it is a lack of ability to make money. Let us focus on information, knowledge and mental empowerment that leads to productivity.

The Orthodox

By my definition, to be orthodox is to be where things were and not where things are. It is a pattern of thinking that hinges on the past, one that is not bold and courageous enough to venture into new grounds and methods of operation. It is mentally living in the past; though physically in the present. It is what we might call being crude or old fashioned.

A mentality of mobility is necessary for productivity

Albert Einstein observed that, "The significant problems we face cannot be solved at the same level of thinking we were at when we created them." We need a new deeper level of thinking: a paradigm based on principles and one which accurately describes the territory of development that reflects true productivity. A wise man said "no one discovers new oceans who is afraid to lose sight of the shore." If we will see change, we must begin to think differently as every lasting change must begin with a mental one. We must first change, if things are to change.

Third World countries and Third World people will remain in the paradox if they continue to be orthodox. We must understand that there are new methods and ways of doing things that are more productive. We cannot remain with outdated technology and want to function in the global arena. Levels of interdependence exist between people and countries. The world is now so mobile and dynamic you cannot afford not to be the same. I love to say that a mentality of mobility is necessary for productivity. Dr Paul Eneche says that the enemy of every revolution is tradition; the enemy of where you should be is where you are. It is time to get acquainted with better systems of governance and production so that we are not left behind by a fast moving world.

A Paradigm Shift

I was told a story as a little boy of a country which sent twelve spies to spy a land they intended to take over and invade. This land had a lot of giants living in it, at least according to situation reports. Ten of the spies returned so scared and intimidated saying "the land is full of giants and we are like grasshoppers before them and will not be able to take the land". This report communicated fear into the hearts of the intending invaders who decided to abort their mission despite the prizes victory would have brought them. However, there were two spies who thought differently. They said their people had what it took to take the land; "the people are bread

To remain orthodox is to remain in your paradox

before us" but unfortunately the majority took the day. The interesting thing about the story is that years later these two spies finally championed a different set of people who saw what they saw and conquered the same country. Is there any challenge before you that seems bigger than you, till you can see yourself overcoming, your mind will not be able to function at a level to devise the way out. If you can believe it, you can do it; nothing is impossible.

Stephen R. Covey once said "We don't see things as they are, we see things as we are." The way we see a problem is a greater problem than the problem itself. The way we see and think could determine whether we succeed or fail. The only difference between the seemingly two exceptional spies is, what others saw as an obstacle to destiny, they saw as an opportunity for destiny.

Every positive shift in perception will lead to a lift in production

A paradigm shift is therefore not only desirable but unavoidable, if we must leave where we are and move to where we could be. The word paradigm, comes from the Greek language. It was originally a scientific term, and is more commonly used today to mean a model, theory, perception, assumption or frame of reference. This term was introduced by Thomas Kuhn in his highly influential landmark book, 'The Structure of Scientific Revolutions'. Kuhn shows how almost every significant breakthrough in the field of scientific endeavour is first a break with tradition, with old ways of thinking, with old paradigms. Every shift in perception will always lead to a lift in levels of production. Change your thinking and watch your life and circumstances change for the better.

In Nigeria today, the CEO of the Daystar Network, Sam Adeyemi is one of the protagonists and pioneers of paradigm shifts. He proposes the law of transformation as a must for any true revolution; either as an individual or on a collective basis. He puts it this way "first within and then without". To allow our outside to shape our inside is breaking the law of sequencing as our inside should shape our outside. I believe that countries are the way they are because of how the citizens are. The state of every country, organisation or family is only a reflection of the state of those in it. If you are not happy with what you are seeing around you, begin to change what you are seeing inside you.

Our paradigms must begin to be based on principles of character and work that enhance productivity. Our paradigms should no longer accept corruption, extremity in political office, armed robbery and cheating which are all incongruous to productivity. We must truly move from dictatorship to democracy, we must allow our constitution to be the baseline for leadership. Transparency and accountability are various paradigm shifts we must make internally. Every true paradigm shift is faced with initial opposition, ridicule, hatred, criticism, then gradual acceptance followed by universal usage and finally commendation.

The sight of your eyes will determine the might of your heart

Paradigms determine our actions, which are the reasons for the way things are in the lives of Third World people and Third World countries. To address our actions without addressing our perceptions will be like shadow boxing; it will be addressing fruits and not roots. Paradigms are inseparable from character. It was

Stephen R Covey who said "Being is seeing in the human dimension." We cannot go very far to change our seeing without changing our being and vice versa. Paradigms are the source of our attitudes and behaviours; we cannot act in integrity outside them. We seemingly cannot maintain wholeness if we walk and talk differently than we see.

Why should I engage in religious and tribalistic fights, killing people of a different faith and language? It is either because I perceive them as enemies or don't value human life at all and see people as animals. Why should a person pick up a gun and rob another? It is because he has not perceived his problem of lack properly; he has allowed his sense of lack to make him feel he is not able to relate with his potential to meet his problem so he behaves in ways unacceptable to normal human behaviour. A man who turns himself into a beggar obviously doesn't have the right perception of himself as he makes himself wholly dependent on others for sustenance whereas in the same environment, people exist who were not born that way but got tired of where they were and picked up responsibility for their lives and destinies. When a man is sleeping when he should be working, something is wrong with his mind. Government officials who amass wealth illegally have the fear of lack in the near tomorrow rooted in their minds. So to be able to continue in a lifestyle they have so enjoyed, they decide to steal. It's all a perception problem.

Imagine what the world would be like today if people like Nelson Mandela or Mahatma Ghandi didn't have paradigm shifts of what good governance is, sparking revolutions that eventually led to lasting changes in their environments. Many blacks live comfortably in America today but people like Rosa Parks and Dr Martin Luther King Jnr paid dearly for it, even risked their lives because they had a paradigm shift to the effect that *difference in colour cannot mean inferiority and slavery*, which led to an infamous indulgence the world will never recover from. Do you see yourself as being poor or rich, down or up, a victim or a victor, a borrower or a lender? Remember it all starts with perception. No matter the condition now it can and will change, only if change can begin from within.

The might of your heart will determine the height of your life

First world countries today are products of a paradigm shift.

The traditional concept of governments for centuries had been a monarchy, the divine right of kings. Then a different paradigm was developed: a government of the people, by the people and for the people. Constitutional democracies were born, unleashing tremendous human energy and ingenuity which invariably led to the creation of a standard of living of productivity, liberty unequalled in the history of the world. A simple shift of paradigms from communism and socialism to capitalism in places like the former Soviet Union has entirely revolutionised the economy. Russia has just about more billionaires than any other country.

In the 1980s, I lived in that part of the world for two years and I can tell you categorically, that particular paradigm shift has led to an industrial and entrepreneurial revolution that has led to individual and corporate expansion. The diagram of every man's life is as a result of his paradigm.

Striking the Match

To postpone your paradigm shift will mean to postpone your productivity. Let me help you to appreciate the boomerang effect of a paradigm shift. Changing your paradigms whether self or social will involve mind renewal. When you renew your mind concerning issues you are actually making things new.

To programme productivity into your life, you must programme your mind with the right stuff

Wow! Isn't it wonderful that you have the opportunity to instill new zeal, character, productivity into your life and work? Take advantage now.

I love the Greek concept of the word renew. In an allegorical sense, it describes a man taking someone by the neck and violently pulling him towards a particular direction and destination. This implies that whenever you want aggressive change, internal or external; self or social; whenever you want to positively change the direction and pace of your life, the right thing to do is to begin to change your perception, i.e. the way you see things. Remember, every action is based on a particular perception. Where do you want to go? Who do you want to be? Begin to take in information from books, articles or any material that will enhance your mental renewal so you can begin to head dramatically towards productivity. Get the right information; associate with the right people and see a positive change of your perceptions.

I conceived the idea for this book when I was just twenty-three years old. I tried to write but failed, due to many hindrances such as a lack of enthusiasm, laziness, my wealth of knowledge and experience at the time. This led to a deferral of the book. At this point, I had given over a hundred public talks but was very dissatisfied with the effect I had made. I only used to write my thoughts on a skeletal plain but was never interested in much writing. This lethargy was actually submerging my potential as it limited my audience and scope of influence. My change however, came when I made my own shift. Two associations were responsible for this.

I met a young lady by the name Ogechi Okeiyi she was at that time a graduate of English and literature from Abia State University. She was a couple of years younger than I and was writing a book on the emancipation of women which was going to be published and released that year. This particular association enforced my paradigm shift as it helped me perceive writing in a more positive light. I suddenly saw the positive effect it could have on my generation and many others to come. My works could get to places I couldn't reach at that time, touching and changing lives. Your association beyond every unreasonable doubt goes a long way to affect your perceptions. I picked up the book again and began to write, that is why I have the privilege of making it available for you to read today. I also came across a poem which enforced my paradigm shift about writing. As simple as the poem may seem, it had a lot of impact on my mind.

Every action is based on a prevalent perception

The world of books
Is the most remarkable creation of man Nothing
else he builds ever lasts Monuments fall
Nations perish
Civilisations grow old and die out
And after an era of darkness
New races build others
But in the world of books are volumes
That have seen this happen again and again
And yet live on
Still young
Still as fresh as the day they were written
Still telling men's hearts
Of the hearts of men centuries dead.
                    Clarence Day

This one poem so articulately and accurately written, short yet so powerful helped me go through a paradigm shift concerning writing. As I write this book, I owe a lot to those two associations and the information gained from them and as I unleash a series of books to help the world in which I live to become a better place. Information and association will always either positively or negatively affect your perception.

Information and association are responsible for shaping your perception

An Example from Bangladesh

Dr Allan Rosefield dean of Columbia University Maiuran School of Public Health asked a group of women from Bangladesh a question. How many of you have five children? No hands went up. Four? Still no hands. Three? One nervous woman looking around, reluctantly put her hand in the air. Two? about 40% of the women. One? Perhaps another 25%. None? The remainder of the women.

A man's outlook on life is tailored by his dominant paradigm

Rosefield then asked how many they want in total? He again started at 5? No hands. Four? No hands. Three? No hands. Two? Almost all hands went up. He had been visiting Bangladesh and other parts of Asia since the 1960s and he remembered vividly the day when Bangladeshi rural women would typically have six to seven children. This is a typical paradigm shift made by these women concerning childbirth. This is indeed a positive shift, as it gives opportunity for the woman to properly attend to her children as well as herself by ensuring proper productivity on both sides. Excessive childbearing is also one of the major causes of poverty. Look around you and see the particular shift you need to make today.

Going Down History Lane

- The great Bill Gates forecast in 1981 said that the personal computer memory of 640 KB ought to be enough for anybody.
- The chief engineer of the British post office said in 1876:

"We don't need a telephone, we have plenty of messenger boys."
- The chief engineer of IBM in 1968 commented about a micro chip, "But what good is it for?"
- Gordon Moore co-founder of Intel said in 1970 that home computers will be a waste of time.
- Both Atari and Hewlett-Packard turned down the idea of a personal computer presented by the developers of Apple and told them to go back to college.

Many examples exist, of events in times past that almost hindered the progress of technology and productivity because men refused to go through a paradigm shift. From the above, you can see that all these men at some point finally went through their paradigm shifts and in so doing realised the possibility of progress. Their new discoveries have now served as catalysts to technological revolutions, they have bettered mankind, and they have bettered our lives. You cannot afford to remain where you are, make the shift in your mind and it will enhance a shift in your life.

CHAPTER THREE:

POTENTIAL AND PROSPERITY

God has without any fear of contradiction endowed every man and every country with what it takes to be productive. To be loaded with so much potential and yet live in abject poverty is a paradox. This is the situation many individuals and countries find themselves in today. There are two routes I describe, one to prosperity and the other to poverty. I provide the solution to the paradox of poverty that countries and people have found themselves in today.

The Diagram of a mans life is tailored by a dominant paradigm

We will be exploring the 5 Ps which will serve as our bridge between potential and productivity. Our soils are loaded with natural resources, our countries are filled with people; the presence of potential is an already established fact. Because potential and performance have not met, it has resulted in several negative situations. This paradox is a contradiction, it is responsible for:

- Frustration
- Depression
- Manipulation
- Oppression
- Confusion
- Recession

Wherever this paradox exists, you will find the above mentioned in manifestations.

1. Principles

Everything in life is powered by principles. Your success, prosperity and all good circumstances you may desire are only possible by principled living. It will be a delusion to believe things can work without paying attention to principles. Every man

When performance is way below potential, frustration is liable to set in

or country that is productive today will tell you they operate by certain principles; you cannot do otherwise. Your decision to become principled is the beginning of accelerated development.

What is a principle:

- A principle is a statement of the way things work
- A high personal standard of what is right or wrong, used to guide behaviour.
- A general rule in which a skill or science is based, which must be understood.

The Face of Principles

1. Principles control results

For every effect there is a cause, a root behind every fruit. We should stop chasing shadows and know what really makes things work. What we need is not what is in the pockets of developed countries but what is in their heads. With principles, you can always reproduce results. Dr

David Oyedepo once said there are no Third World countries only Third World minds. In other words what is in your head will determine whether you will be ahead. Begin to embrace and live by principles and see your life sky rocket to another level. Principles will always make you a principal in your domain.

2. Principles control problems

Many problems we find ourselves with today are as a result of broken principles. We can begin to correct and avoid pitfalls by paying attention to principles. If we relate correctly to problems, facing them with principles, they will surely come under control. Problems always respond to principles. In the Greek language, the word *A problem is a situation which comes to throw you forward* for problem is a composite word Pro—forward, Balai—to throw. In others words a problem is that which comes to throw you forward. With this perception, it is bent to enhance your action. Congratulations! as you begin to relate right with the problems you are facing you will move forward. Remember challenges are the food of champions.

3. Principles are universal

The same principle it takes to bring an individual out of a Third World situation is what it takes to bring out a family, organisation and even a country. There may be certain differences in diversity and applications. What works in Nigeria will work in Ghana, however particular environmental conditions & cultures must be studied to effect proper applications.

4. Principles provide a level playing field

With Principles on the ground no one has an excuse not to be productive. Principles are not biased nor do they discriminate, they provide everyone with a tangible opportunity for success. Embracing them is up to you.

5. Principles make it up to you

There can be no blame game when it comes to success. You cannot excuse yourself or point fingers at your government or leaders. Any assistance you receive from any place can only serve as an instrumental means to productivity; you are at the end of the day the ultimate means for change in your

Live today guarded by principles, they are the womb of tomorrow

situation. You were not responsible for how you were born, but you are responsible for what you become. Ten years from now, you will surely arrive. The question is where? You will surely become. The question is what? Success is by design. Begin to plot and principle your plot then watch yourself metamorphose into that dream person you have always desired to be.

6. Principles make life predictable

There is so much uncertainty in the world today as one government after the other collapses; fear has gripped the hearts of men as nobody seems to know what the future holds. People are no longer confident and look for countries that are seemingly "greener pastures" to settle and build a better life. I would say here that where you live will not matter, where you work is inconsequential unless you decide to live by certain proven principles that are productivity friendly. The principles in this book bring a level of certainty that will help you establish your destiny. You don't have to be confused, scared or remain in the dark about your future.

The world is powered and sustained by principles. If you become principled, you will surely become productive. You can tell the way your tomorrow will become by the way you live today. Today always affects tomorrow as it is the womb in which tomorrow is formed. For our countries to have a future we must begin to respect the principles of people, production, priority and many others I share in this book.

A man who does not save and invest will surely be poor. One who does not work should not expect to eat, if you don't sow, why should you want to reap. If you don't give, you will not receive. When you begin to respect principles you can expect positive results.

Principles are like natural laws that should not be broken; to break principles is to live your life against the tides and you know how difficult that is. The reality of such principles or natural laws becomes obvious to anyone who thinks deeply and examines the cycles of history. These principles surface time and time again, and the degree to which people in a society recognise and live in union with them will move them toward either survival and stability or devastation *If you live by principles, you will* and destruction. *become a principal in life*

As an agricultural economist by initial training, I can categorically say that if we can respect principles and laws half as much as farmers, we wouldn't be where we are today in the Third World. No rational person will argue that corruption, lack of integrity and falsehood are all incongruous to principles that enhance productivity. Principles are simple landmarks that lead to a place of productivity and prosperity. What I am referring to are not complicated, esoteric, abstract or even "mysterious ideas". There is not one principle I express in this book, which can be practiced only by someone in a particular sector belonging to a particular country. Someone once said principles are part of enduring social philosophies and ethical systems. They are self-evident and can easily be illuminated by any individual. They seem to exist deep within all humans, regardless of social conditions, even though they might be silenced by irresponsibility.

2. Purpose

Scientists in the field of human potential have estimated that we use as little as ten percent of our abilities as individuals, families, and organisations. I will show you the connection between potential, purpose and productivity. Dr Myles Munroe defines potential as "All you can be that you have not yet become, all you can do but have not done, how far you can reach but have not reached, what you can accomplish but have not yet accomplished." He goes on to say that potential is "unexposed ability and latent powers".

Purpose is the intention for an invention, the cause of a creation, the essence of existence Based on the productivity principles we should not settle for less. Your family, organisation and country is not yet what it could be. You are more than this; just challenge and channel your potential and create energies in the right directions. I wish to remind us again that these principles can be applied to individuals, families, organisations and countries. This book remains relevant to you notwithstanding where you are. Rick Warren says "To live on purpose is the only way to live, any other thing is simply existing." Every man born of a woman has a purpose to fulfill. As we individually

If you lose sight of your intention for creation, you are heading for frustration

discover and fulfill I our purpose, it now has a collective effect on our countries and helps her "fulfill her own purpose". I define purpose as the intention for an invention, the cause of a creation; the essence for existence. Our involvement in development will remain far-fetched until we understand the concept of purpose. Every country is not the same. There are specific things countries are meant to do based on their available resources and position in terms of geography. When we stray out of our purpose, we face opposition and frustration. Many Third World countries do not know why they exist. We must be known for something. No country can be known for everything. Be it in technology, agriculture, sports or commerce. There are specific areas that we must discover are our strengths and build on them for true and lasting development. Why was I created? Why was I born? Why am I here?

What is it?

1. What is my contribution?

Life is not all about accumulation, it is about contribution. Any organisation or country experiencing distinction in one form or the other is involved in contributing around its environment and to the globe at large. If we must be relevant; it will be because we add value to others. If I must be part of this revolution, it invariably means I am making my own contribution to life out of the potential within me.

The rewards of life are in direct proportion to the value of service offered to others. You don't get something for nothing. Until you are needed in life you will remain needy. The question is who needs you? Who needs your organisation? Who needs your country? Will your absence create a vacuum that will be missed and not easily done without? There are certain people who are pillars; there are some countries that if peradventure vanish today will put the world in chaos because of the place they occupy in the scheme of things based on their contribution to the global community. There is no other way; contribution will always lead to distinction. Begin to look inwards, ask questions and make your life and presence count.

2. What is my communication?

A distinguished Nigerian writer Chinua Achebe said "The Nigerian problem is the unwillingness of its leaders to rise to the challenge of personal example, which is the hallmark of true leadership." Because we have lost sight of the intention for our creation as people; corruption has eaten deep into the fabric of our economies. Character and integrity are now things of the past. Fairness, truth and compassion no more hold sway. It is only a loss of sight in reference to purpose that can make us kill ourselves the way we do, especially in developing nations. No man's destiny and purpose is to be in a

To avert disaster we must all communicate character

particular position. Our purpose is in respect to our function which can be accomplished irrespective of our positions in government and wherever we may find ourselves. Any man who is not conscious of his purpose can be of no good even if he becomes the president of a country. Why do we have people who do not want to leave power? They are there for decades living in self delusion that they own the country. It is simply selfishness and self-deception which are manifestations of people who have lost sight of contribution and communication. What statement is my life making? What is my leadership communicating to others around me? There was once a king in Israel whose leadership made the availability of gold a common thing. His leadership communicated prosperity to the people. What is my life passing across, prosperity or poverty? Our leadership must begin to rethink and do things properly so that generations to come can find a good place to live. Cheating and corruption cannot communicate well to our people. Our lives must begin to speak truth and sincerity as they are necessary ingredients for true productivity.

Third World people, Third World countries, please hear me; we must once and for all settle the identity problem. Dr Myles Munroe once said that

Your identity will enhance your destiny

self acceptance is behind self esteem. We must appreciate our uniqueness, our culture and begin to do things in line with our purpose. John Mason said that imitation is only limitation; every man was born to be an original. The best you can be as a copy is number two. Know yourself, know your country. There is no time to feel inferior. Find satisfaction in your personality and destiny, be who God made you to be. Do what God has empowered you to do and see if you will not be needed because only you can do it like you. You are loaded with potential, you are loaded with resources only connect it to purpose, contribute and communicate and see yourself come out of the pit. Your IDENTITY will always enhance your DESTINY.

3. People

The brother of a very rich and influential man was captured by a particular king. According to this true life story, this influential and rich man at that time was rich in gold, cattle and silver. He also had his own personal army of trained men. One of the servants of his brother happened to escape and brought the news to this rich man; he reacted very quickly by carrying close to four hundred of his trained warriors. He invaded the entire territory of this king, took all his animals, property and people. The king however was spared and left alone. The king, defeated and disarmed returned not much later to this rich and influential man. He had a request to make which he was ready to stake his life for. If this request was not granted he would prefer to die. What was the king's request? He said to the rich man "Keep all my goods, all my cattle and all you took keep, but please give me my people".

To misplace your priorities is to loose your place in life

There is a lesson here that can change the economic situation of every man and country. The king knew that what made him king was that he had people to rule over. He wasn't going to rule over empty land. He understood that the strength of every king is in his people; if you take my people you take my strength; if you take my people you take my kingdom. His priority was not his chariots or his natural reserves. His priority was his people. Every man who will live by misplaced priorities will loose his place in life. This is the problem with Third World people and Third World countries. We think our wealth is our oil (Nigeria), Gold (Ghana) or Diamonds (Liberia). We have looked to the wrong place to find our worth. The true wealth of every country is its people. I love to state that there are three kinds of wealth; money, property and PEOPLE. Until we place the right emphasis on people we will remain in this paradox. Every development is engineered and powered by people; so in effect, the people determine the pace of development. Every country is only a reflection of its people. For example Japan is literally built on water. They do not have the vast natural resources we have in Africa but yet they are doing better. This is because they place emphasis on developing their people mentally. There is a well structured education system which is not just for information but implementation. Their economy works based on the

- PRINCIPLE OF KNOWLEDGE
- PRINCIPLE OF THE MIRROR
- PRINCIPLE OF THE JEWEL

These are all principles directed at the people. Until our leadership realises this and begins to invest in education, technology and passes bills that are people orientated, we will not make much progress. DEMOCRACY is simply a government for the people and by the people. Let us begin to have people directed programmes and in no time the people will positively affect

There are three kinds of wealth; money, property and people

the country. Sometime ago, the British government said Nigerians within the age of 18-30 would not be granted visas as they felt the number of Nigerians in Britain was on the rise. When I heard this, I bubbled with excitement. This however did not go down well with many. I was almost wishing other first world countries would do the same. I usually tell my friends that the Americans had no America to go to; the French had no France to go to. Most developed countries at the time of initial development had no alternative country to go to, so they had to stay and make things work. If you are giving away your potential wealth because of foolishness and the receiver says I don't want anymore, for heaven's sake isn't that a favour? Instead, people began to get jittery and make nasty statements. The answer to our numerous problems is not abroad; the answer is above. Our people are the wealth of our countries, we are the wealth of Africa, we are Africa, we are the world. I love a song by a couple of musicians, I used to listen to it a lot when I was much younger and it illustrates this point very clearly. I'm sure you've heard "We are the world" (sang by several artists) before, the chorus of the song says

WE ARE THE WORLD WE ARE THE CHILDREN
WE ARE THE ONES TO MAKE A BETTER DAY SO
LET'S START LIVING
THERE'S A CHOICE WERE MAKING WE'RE
SAVING OUR OWN LIVES
IT'S TRUE WE'LL MAKE A BETTER DAY JUST YOU
AND ME

This paradigm shift must take place in our governments and organisations. Money should be spent on training as much as possible, to ensure our people are mentally developed enough to change our countries. In our training programmes, we normally say the success of any organisation or country is based on leadership, culture and people. It was Manginal who said that human resource is the life blood of any organisation. Only through well trained personnel can any organisation achieve its goals. Personnel growth and development always leads to productivity, prosperity and profitability of an organisation. Training and developing people should be a strategic focus. We're talking about winning in a highly competitive market. Our objective should be to drive our competitiveness through training. It is not going to happen unless every person makes personal investment in leadership, learning and development. It is not a central concept around building the quality of work life. It is the central concept around moving to the next level. It cannot be over emphasised.

Our leaders in the private and public sectors must make this paradigm shift. Individually, we must begin to invest in the development of our spirits, souls

The success of any country is based on leadership, culture and people

and bodies. Beyond what our countries and organisations will do, we must do even more for ourselves. It is only logical and rational to want to invest anywhere with promise of great returns: you are the place.

- The largest single cost should be PEOPLE
- The largest most valuable asset is PEOPLE
- All business goals will be met or fail to be met by PEOPLE
- Grow the PEOPLE and the PEOPLE will grow the organisation

Remember poverty is not the absence of money; it is a lack of ability to make money. Begin to invest in knowledge, expand your mind, improve yourself,

No one can fetch from the well of prosperity, till he is ready for a stretch

engage in personal development and in no time you will be surprised at what you have the capacity to do. Orison Sweet Marden said "Deep within man dwell those slumbering powers; powers that would astonish him, that he never dreamed of possessing, forces that would revolutionise his life if aroused and put into action." You are more than meets the eye, you are more than people say you are. Begin to challenge, stretch yourself and see yourself perform at a level that will beat your wildest imagination.

4. Production

About 140 BC; in the country of Israel, there was a man who had two sons. They were actually twin brothers. He was one of the biggest farmers of his day, feared and revered by all around him. He seemed to have the ability to beat the odds and succeed where others failed. He grew so large that even other neighbouring countries feared him. As he grew much older, he began to perceive he didn't have much time to live. According to his culture he had the mandate to bless his first twin with the father's blessing. This son was a hunter. The second however was a son of the home, he was more intelligent, he was more involved in mental work as he spent more time at home reading and learning. He was also a very good cook. This great man of industry told the first son to go, hunt and bring back a processed animal for him to eat so he could give him the father's blessing. The eavesdropping mother heard this instruction given to the first son, she quickly alerted the second son who was her favourite and told him to prepare the usual meal the father loves quickly, so he could take the father's blessing before the first son returned. The father being almost blind couldn't recognise the second son as being the second son. He actually succeeded in taking the father's blessing. After sometime, the first son finally came back, but it was too late. His brother had "stolen the blessing".

Before you condemn and pass judgment on the second son, let me tell you something that happened prior to this event. There was a day the first son came back from hunting. On this particular day he was so tired and asked the second son to please give him some food. The younger brother said food I will give you but this I do in exchange for your birthright. The first son allowing his impulse override his reason gave his birth right away such that he couldn't get the father's blessing as a first son.

In this story the first son is the Third World mindset; the second son is the first world mindset. To explain the concept of production from this true life story I must first say that production could be in form of:

- Goods
- Services
- Processing both

The first son had a strong capacity to hunt (physical labour) animals (raw material), but didn't have the mental capacity to take them through a production process to the point of value to man. He had to depend on others to process his kill for him. African countries today have so many natural resources but *To always make a proper decision reason should guard impulse* are still dependent on foreign countries to process them; so they buy from us at cheap rates, process and sell the finished product back to us at higher rates. Our education system must become purposeful in nature to empower the minds of the people to be able to engage in higher forms of technology.

This however does not downplay the importance of natural resources. This is why 80% of the world's resources is controlled by developed industrialised countries which are just 20% of the world's population. To be in control we must begin to engage in production.

When we apply mental work even to the service we give, we will discover new methods and ways to do them better, bringing us into better situations of life. We must become a thinking society. There is no other way.

Producers are always above consumers

No country can come out of this paradox which consumes more than it produces. Who are we indebted to? Consuming countries? No! We are indebted to producing countries because no one lives on natural resources that are not processed. We have to wait for their fuel, gas, their computers, their cars for our sustenance and survival. In Africa today, we are either conscious of consumption or administration (political services) because there are no proper checks and balances in our systems. Corruption is ascending precisely because it seems to be an easy way to get so much money. The richest men in the world today are entrepreneurs. They provide services to their countries because their minds have been processed by training to process goods and services; all the individual contributions of people together with good government structures have led to certain countries becoming first world. What will you give? What will you do? What problems will you solve? Someone said you should be ashamed to die till you win at least one battle for humanity. Any man who doesn't produce anything will remain in a Third World situation; you will become dependent on others to survive. This is not the way God meant it to be. He has put in you something to be someone. Pick up the responsibility; you are up to it.

I have a simple formula to enhance your productive capacity; I call it i4: Information + Inspiration + Imagination + Invention = Production.

i. Information

This is simply acquiring the knowledge necessary to get you ready to perform a task well. It is getting acquainted with what it takes to engage successfully in your trade, assignment or job. There are certain rules of engagement in every system. Simple strategies and methods that increase the quality of work and life. Thomas Edison, the famous inventor once said the first stage of his inventions was studying an average of 1000 articles of his predecessors concerning the particular line of invention he was interested in. Albert Einstein also said: "I feel a sense of debt to those who have gone before me; I am where I am because I stand on the shoulders of my predecessors". There is always a better way: read, ask questions, you do not have to struggle and start afresh; information is the currency of destiny. It determines your purchasing power in the market of life. If you are not rubbing your minds with other bright minds, it will soon become dull. Information to the mind is what food is to the body. If you don't feed your mind with information, it becomes unhealthy and cannot function to take you to your position in life. Get committed, get addicted and watch your life transform.

ii. Imagination

Use your mind and your mind will move your life

This is a high form of thinking. It is the use of the mind till it begins to form pictures inside you. It is simply "IMAGE IN THE IN". Information as it were is raw material for production, it must be processed in the mind for you to get the best out of it. Just as processing gives more value to natural resources, so it does to information. The end result will be a finished product, a finished method or way of doing things which will add value to life. By the imagination of man, he has virtually conquered natural laws. The best inventors, the best artists, script writers will tell you that without the use of your mind to the frequency where it becomes imagination; you will not come out with anything special. Thomas Edison was once asked how he could invent so many things. He said "I think in pictures." Your limitation in life is tied to your imagination. Every genius in his field engages the imaginative faculty of the mind. All things become possible for those who use this part of their mind.

Napoleon Hill in his book 'Think and Grow Rich' talks about two kinds of imaginations. He says the synthetic imagination has to do with simply arranging old concepts, ideas, or plans into new combinations. It creates nothing; it works with material of experience, education and observation. He also speaks of the creative imagination; as the conscious mind working at an exceedingly rapid rate. Any country in distinction today is a product of people who think. I say to Africans begin to use your mind and your mind will move your life. Dr David Oyedepo said "Brainwork is what makes things work." EW Kenyon frequently said, "Make your brain work, it will sweat but make it work, it will improve. It will develop until you become a wonder to those around you." Think through every problem. Conquer your difficulties as part of the day's job.

If you don't get inspired, you are bound to get expired

iii. Inspiration

This is the virtue that is released by powers beyond our realm when we stay long enough in our minds with information. At this point, we begin to come into contact with things beyond our natural selves. We seem to be in contact with the invisible realm. Keep thinking till you get inspired, keep thinking till you find a way through; the answer is available, don't give up. It is at this point you become a wonder to yourself and the world around you. You begin to express rare dimensions of creativity and ingenuity. I believe that this is what happens between the synthetic and creative imagination spoken of above. Don't just think, think through.

iv. Invention

This is that point where distinction becomes inevitable; it makes a star of every country and every man. Do you ever think about the car you drive, the television you watch, the planes you fly in? These things which have made life easier and comfortable did not fall from the skies; they literally fell from the minds of men. Men have discovered new ways of providing better services; you can do the same if you follow these four steps. You will become an inventor in your field, increasing your worth to your world.

Until the germ theory was developed, a high percentage of women and children died during childbirth, and no one could understand why. In military skirmishes, more men were dying from small wounds than from major traumas on the front lines. But as soon as the germ theory was developed, a whole new paradigm, a better improved way of understanding what was happening made dramatic, significant medical improvement possible.

The Newtonian model of physics was a clockwork paradigm and is still the basis for modern engineering. But it was partial, and incomplete. The scientific world was revolutionised by Einstein's paradigm, the famous relativity paradigm which had much higher predictive and explanatory value. The answer to the problem is within you, begin to sink deep into the depth of your being connecting with information and infinite intelligence, drawing out solutions that will make your world a better place to live in.

5. Possibilities

In the bid to connect your potential to the point of real productivity, it would be a mistake to say there will be no contours on such a path of promise. As we fight the battle of underdevelopment and poverty, we are bound to experience certain setbacks; we may find ourselves in dark clouds and valleys. This journey of individual and collective freedom is sure, though not totally smooth. You may have read a book or heard a message like this before and launched out with high hopes, but met hurdles that made you throw in the towel. It is proper for me to prepare you for the battle ahead. It is your vision of possibility that will keep you going. This is one paradigm shift you must make. Come rain, come shine, through thick and thin, prosperity and freedom are sure. Men have fought, men have died fighting, you must believe in your dream enough to die for it. I hope to see you on the other side of the tunnel with your own story of victory. Mathew Ashimolowo of KICC London said "Don't allow what you are going through distract you from where you are going to." Napoleon Bonaparte

Stop saying you cannot because you can

also said "Impossibility: a word only to be found in the dictionary of fools." Norman Vincent Pearle chanted "Knock the 't' off the can't." All things are possible, have a 'can do' mentality and you will end up in productivity and prosperity.

In 1908 for instance, the Wright brothers flew the first aeroplane contrary to the resolution of the Edinburgh society of engineers in 1904 that it was impossible for a metal object to go up in the air. They refused to be limited by what men called impossible and against all odds, they made it happen. A wise man once said "You can, if you think you can." Success or failure depends on whether your thoughts are positive or negative. Every man ends up being a character of his thought life. Your personality is a reflection of your mentality. Don't accept no for an answer. Believe that there is always a way. Begin to fill your mind with positive thoughts and possibilities. Saturate your whole system until you begin to function in a way to make the best of every situation and circumstance. Stop saying you cannot because you can.

CHAPTER FOUR:

PERSONAL FREEDOM

The history of freedom is independence, but the psychology of freedom is intelligence

I will crave your indulgence to be hungry enough for knowledge as you read this chapter, as I take you on a journey from history to psychology and how they are connected with productivity and prosperity. This journey is critical in establishing why we are where we are and finding the way forward. Celebrations on 'independence' days in many countries today have not been total in experience. This is because the machinery of independence has not been fully exploited. We live in a dream world believing that independence from external domination will automatically free us from the shackles of poverty, hunger, disease and corruption. You know as much as I do that the independence of many countries has not brought these about. I intend to an extent, to unmask the machine called independence so we can relate properly with the concept and in the process enjoy all it has the capacity to bring. Independence is a means and not an end in itself, it is meant to first set a country (systems of governance) free so it can set its people free. Many countries have been freed from colonialism and imperialism at least to a great extent, but independence has failed to set the people free. This is not because there is something wrong with the concept but because it has been practiced in isolation. There is a second independence I call "intelligence" that must be weaned into independence to create the kind of effect we expect and want to see. Until a people are free, that country is not truly free. It was Mahatma Ghandi who said "No society can possibly be built on a derail of individual freedom." Nelson Mandela also speaks in this vein saying "To be free is not merely to cast off one's chains, but to live in a way that respects and enhances the freedom of others." Until Africans are free from poverty, Africa is not truly free. The history of freedom is independence but the psychology of freedom is intelligence. True freedom is the combination of independence and intelligence.

Why Freedom
- It creates the opportunity for productivity
- It is the atmosphere for prosperity
- It restores human dignity
- It gives self worth
- It brings serenity
- It is the original intention of God for man.

The great expansionist, Jean Jaques Rousseau said "Man is born free but he goes everywhere in chains." This assertion may be true but it is not totally acceptable. Man has the capacity to fight injustice, poverty, hunger and underdevelopment. There is always a cry from within man when in conditions of bondage

A country is not truly free until its people are free

and limitation to break away because there is placed within each of us an innate desire for freedom.

Going down history lane, many have died, many have been imprisoned, so much blood has been shed in the bid to gain independence. Long periods of riots and wars have taken place and made life unbearable because certain countries fought for independence from external factions and even within countries. Martin Luther King said "Nothing is free, not even freedom." If such a gigantic price has been paid for independence it is only rational to fully explore it so the blood of our past heroes wouldn't have been shed in vain. For true freedom to be won, we must become free from ourselves; the freedom I am referring to is not one that takes knives and guns, it is one that results from the intellectual capacities and powers of man, which when applied, set him free from adverse conditions of life.

The History

Around 550 years ago, voyages of discovery were made by Europeans. This was made possible by better ship designs, new navigation instruments and a crusading wish to search for wealthy colonies which were started in the newly developed lands. The rich countries started to take raw materials from their colonies. The advantage which gunpowder and other technology conferred on them made small European countries control large colonies and kill or make slaves of the people. The purpose of a country was thought to be; to make profit by exporting more and importing less. It had a monopoly of trade with its colonies, and would not allow other nations to trade with them. For every dollar given in aid, three comes back to the rich countries in interest or through debt. African countries are still in poverty and

It is not just about independence, it is about freedom

squalor. It cannot be just about independence, it is about freedom. A wise man said there is nothing in the entire world greater than freedom. I would rather die in abject poverty with my convictions than live in inordinate riches with a lack of self respect.

Countries might no longer be under the influence of colonialism and imperialism in the context of their relationship with other countries but are they still not bound and controlled by the force of hunger and poverty? Many adverse circumstances still prevail in societies today. We must fight to the finish. We must complete the journey of freedom, Africans and all who read this must press beyond the boundaries of being controlled by countries to the point where we are not controlled by circumstances. It is a realm where man gets into a certain level of freedom based on his level of productivity. Having taken an excursion into the history of freedom, let us peep into the psychology of freedom which is the missing power link to our prosperity as individuals.

The Psychology

The history of freedom is independence; the psychology of freedom is intelligence. When intelligence is coalesced into independence, the end product is prominence. From observations and several researches, I have discovered that countries and individuals, who are prominent, operate based on these two critical factors.

Intelligence may be broadly defined as a facility for solving problems. Such facility is usually related to the competencies described in cognitive social theories and behavioural genetics. What I will be presenting can literally turn your life right side up.

It has the capacity to change the education system for the better, getting people properly prepared for a life of productivity during and after school. It will point the way to true productivity and prosperity.

Until this century, the word intelligence has been used primarily by ordinary individuals in effort to describe their own mental powers as well as those of other persons. Intelligence cannot be conceptualised, or measured with accuracy, independent of the particular context in which an individual happens to live, work, play and of the opportunities and value provided by that milieu. Man's intellectual capacity is that part he uses to approach problems and create products. Psychologists over the years have had certain conflicts on this issue. The understanding of this concept will bring any individual and country out of a Third World situation. I will however take us a little through the works of certain psychologists. By so doing, you will be able to locate your particular sphere of operation, and how to step up to a higher environment for better results.

The fight over intelligence has been about the existence of singular or multiple intelligence modules in the mind.

Not to develop your intelligence, is to say no to prominence

Researchers such as LL Thurnstone and JP Gailferd argued that intelligence was better conceived as a set of possibly independent factors. Development psychology and neology including a number of investigators have put forth the view that the mind consists of several independent modules, or "intelligences". Movements on the intelligence trend show no sign of abating.

Proponents of one general intelligence (GI)
- Binet
- Gatton
- Spearman
- Jensen

Proponents of multiple intelligences (MI)
- Gardner
- Sternberg
- Thurston
- Wallace and Wing
- Eysneck

I will briefly point out the postulations of two psychologists from each group and then we may see the way forward.

Binet (GI)

Binet was an educational psychologist, actually a physician by training, who around the turn of the century founded the French School of Intelligence Testing that has come to dominate intelligence testing world wide (Eysneck & Eysneck 1985). Binet was interested in finding students who were mentally handicapped

Intelligence + Independence = Freedom

and "uneducable" and to remove them from public schools. This Binet's concern with intelligence testing was highly practical and relatively theoretical. The composite score of an individual on a Binet—style intelligence test is called an intelligence quotient, or IQ. A psychologist at Stanford University revised Binet's original test, and this revision became the now classic Stanford-Binet, the model for nearly all intelligence testing including, college and graduate school admissive test like SAT, EMAI, SSCE, GCSE, 'A' LEVELS, MCAY, LSAY).

Spearman

In 1904, Spearman came up with what he called the positive manifold. The positive manifold implies that scores on a vocabulary test will correlate positively with scores on a mathematical test. Therefore, it is unimportant which tests are used to assess general intelligence, they will correlate highly anyway (the principle of indifference of the indicator).

Wallach and Wing

Wallach and Wing (1969) found that scores on a scholastic test (SAT) predict classroom achievement but not achievement in extracurricular pursuits such as leadership, writing, science and art. Achievements in these fields depend a lot also on ideational productivity or effort. "Cognitive vitality" or energy may be more important predication of talent than intelligence.

Sternberg

In 1985 Sternberg developed a theory of intelligence with three components; analytical (academic), creative and practical intelligence.

Analytic Problems	Practical Problems
Clearly Defined. Comes with one right answer. Comes with all information needed to solve problems. Formulated by other people, Disembodied from ordinary experience	Poorly Defined. Several acceptable answers. Requires problem recognition and formulation. Embedded in and requires prior ordinary experience.

There is one more proponent of intelligence that I will present. It is more explicit and encapsulating than the rest of them. All other theories of intelligence seem to handle the concept from a partial point of view. However Sternberg, Wallach and Wing make critical points on understanding man's performance in life. Howard Gardner seems to be more explicit in his concept. His theory of intelligence would set any man on the path to personal freedom. It would enhance African emancipation from starvation. I will however add little modifications and be more explicit on his concept to help your understanding. Howard Gardner presents seven intelligence modules.

1) Intra-personal Intelligence
2) Interpersonal Intelligence
3) Spatial Intelligence
4) Musical Intelligence
5) Bodily Kinaesthetic Intelligence
6) Linguistic Intelligence
7) Logical Mathematical Intelligence.

When you are not in your flow, you will be slow

I will take the liberty to group these seven modules of intelligence into three categories.

Dummy Intelligence

1. Intra—personal Intelligence

This is the intellectual capacity to look deep within yourself to discover your strengths and weaknesses. At this level, you become familiar with your gifts and talents, your natural flow and preferences. One of the reasons people are in poverty is because they have not taken the journey of self—discovery to know where they fit in life and destiny. God has deposited a gift, a particular intellectual power that is meant to be the instrument for your liberty from poverty. Nobody is cut out for everything. When you are not in your flow, you will be slow in life.

This is the ability to consult with yourself to know yourself. This is where the journey begins. If you miss it here, you will be disobeying the natural order and will pay dearly for it. No matter how you love football, not everybody can play football, not everybody can be an engineer. Know what your gifts are, it will give your life a lift. Self discovery always leads to recovery. Many struggle through school and life because they are doing what they aren't wired for. When you are wired for a thing you are always excited and you do not easily get tired. Every day is exciting; you look forward to your job. Why is Monday the worst day for many people? They dread going back to 'THAT' job. Money is a good motivation for work, but in the long run you will soon discover that it is not enough. Man is not designed to be at his best when he does things he is not naturally wired for. If you can identify with what I'm saying, do not leave your job just yet. Make sure you have a well set out plan. Begin to create systems in arenas of your talent and you will soon have the freedom to do just the things you love.

This is a dummy because everybody must develop this kind of intelligence. You might not have other intellectual capacities but you must have this one. No one attains prominence outside his peculiar intelligence, look at yourself in the mirror, reintroduce yourself to you and watch a new level of production come out of you.

You easily get tired when you do what you're not wired for

General Intelligence

2. Interpersonal Intelligence

This is the ability to relate with another person and get along. We have already established the need for people either as mentors, instructors, friends, angels, and subordinates in life. Life is all about a chain reaction of several relationships, no man can make it on his own. Two is always better than one and there is a better reward for their labour. Many businesses and organisations have lost customers due to poor human relations, many people have lost their angels because they couldn't relate properly. Developing this intellectual capacity will enhance your productivity. Every man needs somebody at some time. You need people to complement your weaknesses. That is what makes a man look totally strong. People with this kind of intelligence never lack helpers; they have an aura around them that is attractive to others. They know what it is, to be grateful, respectful and thankful. They possess a sense of intelligence that people want to be around. Your business cannot grow without people. As you begin to develop skills in human relations, by reading books, attending seminars and by practice, you will notice more energy and speed in your life and destiny as input comes from all directions. Your prevailing attitudes can either attract or repel people from you. Begin to fix your attitude and watch them change your altitude.

Specific Intelligence

3. Spatial Intelligence

This is the intellectual capacity to think and draw pictures. Some people have a natural flair for architecture, fine art, fashion and design. If you know you have this flair, settle down, study this area and grow in it. It is a man's gift that makes room for him and brings him before great men. A wise man once said, "A gift is a precious stone in the eyes of him that has it: wherever it turns, it prospers." Turn the knob on your gift, it will trigger your shift. Do not be carried away by the writers, speakers or even sportsmen. Stay on your course, stay focused and you will soon become a shining star. Anyone who stands out has discovered his areas of strength and stayed there. If what you read in school is not your flair begin to constructively plan your movement to your natural arena. Don't just leave your job and stay idle, that is foolishness. Have a plan of action, get the next job, create that business, watch it for a while, then based on the results you can make a concrete decision on the next step to take before leaving where you are now.

Turn the knob on your gift, it will trigger your shift

4. Musical Intelligence

I would love to say at this point that no intellectual capacity is inferior to another. Each one has its own ability to liberate anyone from poverty. This kind of intelligence manifests in areas such as singing, playing of instruments, musical production and so on. Some musicians went to formal schools, some did not. One of my artists, who is presently working on an album (at the time this was written), has made it clear to me that he wants to go back to university after the album is released. He wants to study computer science as he believes it will also help facilitate his dream of producing his own music, and I'm totally behind him. Make sure you do not act in isolation. Ask questions, for in the multitude of counselors there is safety.

So many people have come out of poverty through this intelligence. In fact the entertainment industry today is a lot more financially rewarding, than a lot of the so

You are the money you are looking for

called white-collar jobs. Hundreds of thousands of people flock to musical concerts and pay gate fees, just to watch musicians perform. The sound guru Yanni makes millions of dollars from a concert just by a unique combination of sounds from different instruments. There are musically inclined people all over the world, the list is endless. They bring joy to the soul with their songs, they solve problems; at least at that plain of life. Don't let anyone discriminate against you. Develop your gift and walk in the light of it. It is God's endowment to equip you to be useful in life and destiny. To ignore it, is to ignore your prosperity. However, I still recommend a level of formal training at least in the line of your natural flair, as it will give you the opportunity to exercise your intellectual capacities for growth and progress.

5. Bodily Intelligence

This refers to the intellectual capacity of body movement. It is the ability to move the body to entertain and to play sport. Musicians who have this intellectual capacity usually have an edge over their competitors as they dazzle their audience with good music and dance steps. Artists like Michael Jackson, Usher, p2, Bobby Brown all have bodily kinaesthetic intelligence. Ballet dancers, footballers and basketball players all exhibit this particular intelligence. Many have eradicated the epidemic of poverty from their lives by using this intellectual power. I would like to say here that you can exhibit more than one of the specific intelligence modules. That will mean more responsibility because when much is given, much is expected. However, even if you have just one it is more than enough to take you to the top; it is more than enough to bring in productivity and prosperity. Stop running helter skelter. You are the money you are looking for. Instead of being carried away by the other intelligence modules of others, develop yours to the point of expertise where others would want to be like you and be where you are.

Conformity is an abuse to identity

6. Linguistic Intelligence

This is the intellectual capacity for languages. It could be written or verbal. This is where public speakers and authors come into play. It is the ability to communicate information in written or spoken form to inspire and motivate. This is one of the areas I am good at. When you operate from your place of strength, you seem not to have any weaknesses. You seem to be so whole and perfect. Don't expose your ignorance and foolishness by trying to do what you're not cut out for. It is the manifestation of various "intelligences" in a society that gives it its wholeness. If you refuse to be you, who will be you? Conformity is an abuse to your identity which is where your productivity and prosperity lies. Men like Anthony Robbins, Zig Ziglar, Les Brown all function using this intellectual capacity.

> *True freedom is not one that involves weapons of war, it is that which results from using intellectual capacities of man for productive causes*

7. Logical Intelligence

This has to do with numbers. I have never really liked mathematics and have always preferred courses which I need to read. There are some people who get turned on by figures. Accountants, auditors, mathematicians all have and use this particular intellectual capacity.

I would like to add another group.

8. Intuitive or Spiritual Intelligence

I believe that God has made it possible for everyone to have a flourishing relationship with Him. However, there are a set of people who dedicate themselves wholly to spiritual service. They seem to have an extraordinary relationship with the unseen world and have the ability to carry others into a similar relationship. These are the ones that have very strong contacts with divinity and they communicate the same. Nothing can satisfy those in this category other than bringing divinity into the realm of humanity. Seeing God's work in the life of man is what they live for. They are filled with revelations about the unseen realm, about how man can relate with that realm to secure his destiny here on earth. They are usually known for demystifying spiritual truth, in a way that ordinary men can comprehend. In a nutshell, it is the ability to be in contact with God, understanding how he speaks and following his lead.

'Miscellaneous Intelligence'

I am very aware of the fact that these modules may not cover all aspects of talents and gifts in a man's life. However, they do give a broad view. That is the reason for this last postulation. Do a proper self-consultation, and you will discover more of yourself, as the machine called man is so diverse and complicated. It is almost

When you discover your intelligence, develop, direct and deal it

impossible to keep him in a box as he seems to evolve with new skills and abilities with the passing of time. It could be cooking, entrepreneurship or even leadership that is your own area. Whatever it is, that is where your freedom from poverty lies. That is where you can be truly productive. Stop complaining and start working. I will give you four of my prescriptions in the context of intelligence.

What to do with your intelligence

- Discover it,
- Develop it,
- Direct it and
- Deal it.

If you have carefully read to this point you should have met with yourself by now. Step out of yourself in your mind and take a look at yourself. Take notice of the things that turn you on, the problems you want to solve, your skills and abilities, they are all pointers to your particular intelligence.

After you discover, begin to develop. When you develop your intelligence, it becomes skill. It can now be of use to society. No matter what nature bestows you with, you must be willing to nurture it to establish your future. Your gift will not just exude; you must work at it, to make it work. Your gift is like sugar at the bottom of a tea cup, until it is stirred, its effect will not be felt. It will take work and time but the results will be worth it all.

Develop it by use and exercise. Give it attention. As your muscles begin to ripple so will your productivity. Any man who seems to stand out has spent many nights bending down. A wise man once said a boxing champion is not made in the ring, he is only discovered there. The early morning jogging, exercises and rehearsal fights all contribute to the process.

You must direct your intelligence. You must create space for it to find expression. You must also identify your target audience. Not everybody will want what you have. Writing this book for instance is creating space for my writing ability to be released. The seminars I hold provide me with the opportunity to speak; the various network of public speakers also provides this opportunity. As I write this page, I will be speaking in a behavioural change conference in less than twenty-four-hour's time organised by a friend who is also a public speaker.

When you nurture what nature has given to you, you are establishing your future

You must also sell your intelligence. There is nothing like something for nothing. Take it to the market place. If it solves a problem, put a price tag on it and men will pay for your product. Remember the history of freedom is independence and the psychology of freedom is intelligence. I will close this chapter with a speech that shook the foundations of America. It was given by a freedom fighter, one whose life has brought inspiration and motivation to many. He used his Linguistic intelligence to spark a revolution. This popular speech "I have a dream" was given by a young, black Baptist preacher Martin Luther King.

The law of every true kingdom is freedom

"I am happy to join with you today in what will go down in history as the greatest demonstration for freedom in the history of our nation.

Five score years ago, a great American, in whose symbolic shadow we stand today, signed the Emancipation Proclamation. This momentous decree came as great beacon light of hope to millions of Negro slaves . . .

But one hundred years later, the Negro is still not free . . .

. . . One hundred years later, the Negro lives in a lonely Island of poverty in the midst of a vast ocean of material prosperity.

. . . Let freedom ring from the prodigious hilltops of New Hampshire. Let freedom ring from the mighty mountains of New York let freedom ring . . . .

As we journey in the spirit of freedom both individually and as a country we must be ready to break through the barriers of laziness, corrupt leadership and violence. Our desire should ignite such a fire that we become unstoppable. You are made for the top. You are made for prosperity; you only need to work at it. Remember independence and intelligence will lead to personal freedom.

PART TWO

POWER AND PROSPERITY

*"It takes power to build a tower:
energy to establish a destiny"*

CHAPTER FIVE:

TWO POWER LINKS TO PROSPERITY

I wish to remind us at this point that poverty is not the absence of money but the absence of the ability to make money. It is a lack of productivity. The message is quite very simple; stop, looking into your pocket and start looking into your head. The question is what do you know about what you have (Potential)? How much of it have you developed and channeled into your environment? This is God's gift to mankind to enable him to better his life. No man or country will come out of this paradox till he learns to understand, maximize and release his potential. Every time you reach into your potential to reach out to your world you are bound to get relevance alongside riches. My prescription therefore to developing countries, development agencies and to mankind in general, is to ensure that they don't get carried away with funds from international institutions forgetting the issue of human resource development which is a prerequisite for community development. Personal development as I prescribe is an aphrodisiac to productivity which is the answer to poverty.

Whenever you reach into your potential to reach out to your world, you are bound to come across relevance and riches

Even though there are different perspectives to development, there is a general consensus that development will lead to good change manifested in the increased capacity of people to have control over material assets, intellectual resources, ideology and to obtain physical necessities of life (food, clothing and shelter), economic independence, adequate education and gender equality. This is why some people have argued that the purpose of development is to improve lives by expanding their choices, freedom and dignity. I am simply drawing your attention to the development of your potential to make your environment better, which will lead to personal empowerment, enhancing further community development.

Nigeria was one of the richest countries in the early 1970s and is now among the twenty-five poorest countries in the world despite its natural and human resources. If you can relate with this or you are committed to changing such situations around the globe, I am about to prescribe one ingredient that when applied will bring you into a high level of productivity, eradicate poverty to the barest minimum and result in a first world situation.

Building the bridge between potential and productivity is bridging the divide between the rich and poor. You must

Power connected is progress initiated

intentionally and consciously cross my bridge for my prescription to enforce liberation into your life and country. Potential always produces confidence and confidence is knowing potential is there. This is why I know assuredly that as you apply this prescription, you are bound to experience change.

My sixth 'P' for productivity is power. Everything and everyone survives and is sustained by one form of power or another. Plants, animals, living and non-living things all exist because of the release of power. To move from one point to another, all you need is the application of power. The presence of power is the presence of progress. You cannot stop making progress when you are connected to a source of power. I am about to wire you up to this source, so you can begin to experience a new kind of energy to power you to your next level. No "tower" can be built without "power". The word power simply means:

- Faculty of the human personality
- Strength or force
- Ability, strength to do or act.

Nothing works by watching. Things work by powering; nothing moves till you make it move, nothing happens till you make it happen, enough of wishing and hoping. It is time to start acting.

To move from one spot to the other, you will require the application of power

I wish at this point to introduce you to my circle of power. As you journey within, without through these sixteen dimensions, you are bound to experience more power than you have ever dreamed of to move what needs to be moved and change what needs to change. Power is available, be open minded and you will connect.

Circle of power (1)

1) Powered by Mentality
2) Powered by Strategy

1. Powered By Mentality

Every development, advancement and achievement recorded in human history came as a result of a thinking mind. As I have stated earlier, the state of any country is a reflection of the state of the people in that country. Therefore, a Third World country is a place predominantly occupied by Third World people and a Third World person, is a person with a Third World mind. The root of our problem therefore, is the state of our minds. I challenge you to mental development as it will increase your value as a person and inevitably your country. When mentality is mixed with activity we are bound to get productivity. If you don't use your mind, you are going to remain behind. Propel your life forward by simple mental activity. John Mason once said that "You don't always have to work harder, sometimes you just need to work smarter." Let's begin to work with our heads and not just our hands; it will increase the worth of our work and our world.

Your worth in life is only a function of your contribution to mankind. Your importance is a product of impact. There

If you don't use your mind you will be left behind

is always a better way to do what you are doing now. There is a way out of that problem even thought it looks Herculean in size. Begin to think, begin to reason, look within the potential of your mind and combine it with information then, see yourself come out with answers to the problems in your world making it better and bigger, and inevitably taking you to a point of relevance and riches.

Meet Your Mind

I remember reading a scientific report which said the human brain is a *vast network of intricate machinery through which the power of thought is translated into its material equivalent.* Men of science are continuously studying this thing called the brain. It has been determined that there are from 10,000,000,000 to 14,000,000,000 nerve cells in the human cerebral cortex and we know that these are arranged in definite patterns. These arrangements are not haphazard. They are orderly. Recently developed methods of electro-psychology draw off currents from very precisely located cells, or fibres with micro-electrodes, amplify them with radio tubes and record potential differences to a millionth of a volt.

It is alarming and mind blowing that such a network of intricate machinery could be in existence for the sole purpose of enhancing man's life here on Earth. To have such power in us and yet live so helplessly is unfair to us, our potential and to the One who gave it to us. With such inherent power man can literally do and be anything. Someone said more gold has been mined from the minds men than the earth itself. Are you not challenged when you see how far ahead the world has gone, some men and countries are so superior, they seem to have left others behind? Please stop staring at life so quizzically, it is not so difficult, no one has two heads, some just use theirs more. Use your brain and be on the train to success.

The word mentality refers to the attitude of our minds; it deals with our pattern and flow of thought. The right orientation is bound to enhance your creation. If things are right within; they will end up right without. I will be describing five kinds of mentality at this point.

1) Informed Mentality
2) Trained Mentality
3) Inspired Mentality
4) Positive Mentality
5) Creative Mentality

1. Informed Mentality

Ralph Waldo Emerson said "What lies behind us and what lies before us are tiny matters compared to what lies within us." The men we call genius today are men who poured work into certain areas of their lives so much that these areas now distinguish them. One of the areas of discipline common to uncommon men is the acquisition of information. If you are too lazy to read, you will never be able to experience the full capacity of your mind, life will remain hazy. The mind in itself is only potential but when you put in information it activates it and begins to process and produce leading to productivity. When you don't know a better way you cannot get a better result. Bill Gates just didn't become a computer whiz kid and millionaire at the age of twenty-one. History has it that at the age of sixteen, Bill had read almost everything he could read on computers. He started Microsoft at the age of nineteen with Paul Allen. Anthony Robins, a multimillionaire motivational speaker comments that most people have no idea of the great capacity we command when we focus all of our resources on mastering a single

Not to know what you have, is not to use what you have. Not to use what you have is to abuse what you have

area of our lives. Tony didn't have a college degree but by the age of eighteen he had read over seven hundred books, today he is CEO of a fleet of companies and one of the most sought-after speakers in America today. Abraham Lincoln once said "I have no respect for a man who is not wiser today than he was yesterday." Begin to cooperate with your mind and give it what it needs to move you to the next level. Information will always lead to:

- Distinction
- Expansion
- Transformation and
- Translation.

There are many other benefits to gaining information. Your level of information is your limitation. Break away from the limits and do what you were born to do and be who you were born to be, but remember life responds to principles. JF Kennedy once said "Anyone who stops learning is old either at twenty or eighty but anyone who keeps learning stays young." The greatest thing in life is to keep your mind young. That is keeping your mind open to new information that will help generate commensurate results. The world we live in is a changing world, we must keep pace with current knowledge. If the information at your disposal is obsolete, then it cannot produce any current results. Tradition, as is popularly said, is the worst enemy of civilisation because it has no regards for current knowledge. A wise man also said that you will be the same that you are this year in five year's time, except for two things: the books you read and the people you interact with. Get tired of where you are and begin to power your mind to power your life.

2. Trained Mentality

To train means:

- To teach to perform a particular skill or job well
- To behave in a particular way by regular instruction and practice
- To make one's mind quick to perceive things
- To make something or someone grow in a particular direction
- To make someone or something fit to function
- A sequence of connected thoughts and events.

Mental activity leads to mind-blowing creativity

Every man remains far from his best at his job, until he is trained. To work and perform in certain areas you must be trained. A professional cannot be better than the training he has undergone either as an individual or in a group. This could take a formal or informal approach. As scintillating as the capacity of the mind may be, to function at its peak, it must be trained.

Every man who seems to be a genius has gone through series of mental training in the area of his interest. A doctor's mind functions differently, from that of a geologist or a banker. When a sculpturist sees a stone he begins to see a picture inside the stone, something he can carve out of worth and beauty. A builder will probably see the stone as raw material for his building project, a geologist will want to grind it to powder and find out its components. These various perceptions are based on the different trainings each mind has received.

A trained mentality is beyond an informed mentality. It is acquisition of information towards a particular direction. When I talk about the power of information I do not mean you should just read haphazardly in a zig zag manner; you will not properly train your mind in that way. It involves purposeful education, reading and studying around a particular area or issue. To train your mind, you must calendar your development; you must have a target and a schedule. Formal educational institutions provide a system that enhances a trained mind. This could, however, be done by an individual. To function as a CID or FBI agent there is a kind of training you must go through. For your mind to produce beyond its current level it must be trained. The mind has a feedback mechanism. It operates by the law of repayment dynamics. To experience its capacity, you must programme it to perform. This involves reading, thinking, synthesising, practising memory and analysing. Give your mind some exercise so it can be fit, to fit you in your place in destiny. As you begin to exercise your mind in a particular direction you will be amazed at the efficacy of the feedback mechanism.

3. Inspired Mentality

The brain of man is not just to be carried. When properly used it can literally carry man

This involves a sudden idea that dawns on one in the process of thinking. It is a process of events that stimulate the faculties of the mind to perform. Isn't it surprising that we are told that all the advancement in development around us is just a result of man using about ten percent of his mental capacity? As we increase the mind's capacity, we increase our capacity for productivity. Thomas Edison said "To become a genius: it takes one percent inspiration and ninety-nine percent perspiration." However, it is important to understand this vital concept of inspiration since it has a part to play in production.

Respecting the law of progression and sequencing; for any mind to enjoy inspiration it must first be informed and then be trained. The Greek word for inspiration is theopneustos which means for God to breathe. It refers to the assistance we receive from the unseen realm concerning our work to help us perform at our very best. Songwriters, film makers and even preachers usually function at this level of mentality. At this point you function at a level beyond the normal and average. You can move up the ladder, you can be among the upper echelon in your place of work: just begin to programme your mind for productivity.

4. Positive Mentality

The mind of man is like a magnet. Positive thoughts that are prevalent in it attract positive people and positive experiences. Negative thoughts do the same. Third World countries don't need people who cannot see beyond their noses. They need people who can see beyond the dark clouds, through the tunnels to the other side of light. When you are negative about your life and country, your mind is not productive at a level to fashion out solutions to your problems, but remaining positive will affect your thoughts, talk and actions. They will all be tailored towards making things work and history has it that man can always achieve what he puts his whole being to achieve. What is that situation that seems impossible? Have you lost hope? As long as it is a worthy cause I can assure you: stay bold, stay

Not to be positive is to become a fugitive

courageous, stay positive and allow your mind to work in your favour. Ralph Emerson once said that you will learn great things come out by right thinking; life becomes what we think. If things must be right, our thinking must be right. This is a principle that cannot be broken. If you go down history lane you will learn that every man who achieved anything worthwhile had a strong unwavering conviction concerning his destination. Centuries ago Guatama Buddha said "The mind is everything. We become what we think." The Roman Emperor and philosopher Marcus Aurelius declared "Our life is what our thoughts make it." William James, turn of the century professor of philosophy and anatomy at Harvard University, said "The greatest discovery of my generation is that human beings can alter their lives by altering the attitudes of their mind." "Our expectation not only affects how we see reality, but also affects reality itself" says Dr Edward James, a psychologist at Princeton University. I have given all these references by men of authority in their fields to further buttress my point. To have positive experiences you must first have positive thoughts. Begin to literally brainwash yourself, decongest your mind from anything that makes you lose faith, to think and speak negatively.

This is so important, because the way we feel is connected to the way we think. Man has been created in such a way that if he is negative in his thinking, he will before long begin to feel that way. This feeling of negativity drains you of energy, creativity and enthusiasm. All the emotion you need to work your way into the situation you desire is taken away. Even your mind shuts down the moment negative thoughts are prevalent. It can no longer function at a certain level to devise means and methods of progress. If you must stay afloat, you must stay positive.

5. Creative Mentality

The right orientation will always inspire creation

I love to describe the mind of man metaphorically as soil. Every farmer knows the importance of the soil to his harvest as a farmer. The soil must be right and properly nurtured to produce properly. If the farmer plays around with the principle that governs soil productivity, he is bound to be poor. Although the soil is a necessary factor in productivity, it must relate well to other factors of production such as seeds, water and temperature to ensure a good yield. What seeds are to the soil, information is to the mind. Information is always pregnant with more information. It has the capacity to reproduce when sown into the mind, given the right conditions. People who function in this realm of mentality are usually regarded as geniuses.

The whole process of outlining types of mentality is intended to illustrate the right mental atmospheric conditions for the mind as man's inherent potential to function at a certain level, powerful enough to change his position for the better. To be creative involves skillful and imaginative use of the mind. Every man has creative instincts in him; you just need to develop them. At this level you will always relate with your environment to come out with new ways of doing things and impressive results. You are a co-creator with God: begin to live it.

To explore the concept of creative mentality a bit further, we will look into the Hebrew meaning of the word create. Out of the many definitions of this concept, we will view just two: Bara and Asah. Bara simply connotes creating something out of nothing. It has a profound metaphoric significance. It is usually expressed using scientifically precise language and connotes spontaneous creation. Your situation or that of your country may seem as though nothing good can come out of it, but I beg to differ. There are creative instincts in you. Begin to task your mind and watch it feed you with answers that will literally blow your mind. This also tells us your thoughts which are invisible, intangible and seem as though there is nothing physical to be worked on or processed, can become something worthwhile. From zero you can become the hero, you can move from pain to gain, from shame to fame, from a nobody to somebody desired by everyone; many have proven it, they have walked on the path of creativity and experientially moved toward unending productivity and prosperity. You are next in line. Don't disappoint your country, organisation and family. You have the answer. Look deep within and begin to draw it out.

Any man who achieves anything worthwhile, must have a strong conviction concerning his destination

Many times, when we talk about inventions, creations, science and technology, many get discouraged and erroneously believe that it is not for them but only for a select, gifted few in that area. I beg to change your perception. What may be needed are small but important changes that do not call for much technical expertise.

The second Hebrew word we will explore Asah; makes this very clear. It describes the most common of human activities. A better way of talking to your spouse, better human relationship skills, writing a better business proposal, a more effective way of using your time and so on. It also connotes making something out of something.

You don't have to reinvent the wheel all over again, Bill Gates didn't invent the computer; he just came out with better programs and softwares. You can improve what someone else has already done. Put in your uniqueness and originality and watch your productivity increase.

2. Powered by Strategy

Where there is no strategy, you are bound to face agony

Every man's perception of life determines his response and relationship to life itself. If you view life as a race, you will be conscious of speed and breaking speed records; a view of life as a game will produce a winning mentality. There are many allegoric perceptions necessary to relate with life in a productive manner. At this point however, I will look at life as a war field. Having a dad who was in the military I grew up appreciating the armed forces. I attended a military high school. The delicacy of military operations produces a set of disciplined and articulate people.

The concept of strategy cannot be over-emphasized if we want productivity in our lives. No individual or country can fight poverty

It is a daydream to expect prosperity without strategy

without a laid out strategy and expect to win. A strategy is simply a plan defined for a particular purpose, a process of planning out something or carrying out a plan in a skilful way. It could also be referred to as the act of directing military activity in a battle or war. Things don't just happen, they must be powered to happen. Anything you cannot win on paper, you cannot win on the ground. To effect change in our situation, we must first sit down and draw a plan of action. Where there is no strategy you are bound to face agony and tragedy. Dr David Oyedepo, the Chancellor of the Covenant University in Nigeria and President of the Winners World says that planning gives value to your time, resources, and ultimately to your pursuits. It is the non—transferable responsibility of everyone who desires true success. He goes on to state that planning is nothing but the application of logical, rational and analytical thinking to your objective. You will never know the worth of what you have until you are committed to planning. To a non-planner, nothing is enough, nothing is sufficient or adequate.

What strategy have you devised to come out of where you are and to move to the next level? It is a daydream to expect prosperity without strategy. Success is not by accident, it is by design. Begin to gather relevant information about what you want, find out what it takes to get there and begin to lay down a step by step action plan to get you to your destination.

Many countries today have come up with their own poverty reduction plans

- Ghana's Poverty Reduction Strategy (GPRS)
- Uganda's Poverty Eradication Plan (PEAD)
- Ethiopian Sustainable Development and Poverty Reduction Program (SDPRP).
- Kenya's Economic Strategy for Wealth and Employment Creation.
- Nigeria's National Economic Empowerment Development Strategy (NEEDS)

Then there is also the New Partnership for African Development (NEPAD)

Remember that the same principles required to enhance the productivity of an individual can be applied on a bigger scale, though it may require more technicality and professionalism. Having a strategy may not be all it requires to fight poverty, but it is an ingredient that we cannot do without in this fight. Monitoring and evaluation must be put in place to further enhance productivity and prosperity. Don't be in hurry to run. To run without a plot is to flop. Time spent in devising a strategy is not wasted time. Indeed it will save your time, money and energy. It was Abraham Lincoln who said "If I have ten hours to cut a tree, I will spend six hours sharpening my axe." The time spent creating your strategy is to ensure that you realise your purpose and pursuits.

Don't be in a hurry to run, to run without a plot is to flop

Jeffrey Sachs in his book, "An End to Poverty" proposes certain factors that must be present in a poverty reduction strategy:

- A differential diagnosis
- An investment plan
- A financial plan
- A donor plan
- A public management plan.

Understanding Strategy

1. Have the big picture in mind

This is knowing what you want, and where you are and where you want to go. It involves being long-term minded not short-term minded. This will help you stay focused and avoid distractions on your way to your destination. Many times, the desire for 'quick fixes', instant gratification does not allow us pave the way for true success. Every plan of action has phases. Each phase must be properly handled before moving to the next one. This helps you balance

War without target is a war with regret

your activities. Thus, you know when to save, when to spend and when to invest.

2. Have the end picture in mind

If you are going nowhere you will end anywhere. War without a target is war with regret. This will help you measure progress as all activity does not lead to productivity. This helps you to aim for your bull's eye. You can know when victory has been won. Challenges are bound to arise on the way but fixing your mind on the end picture will keep you motivated and excited.

3. Have the way picture in mind

There is always a road map to any destination. There are many roads that do not lead to "the place". Without finding out the way, you could spend time and energy on the wrong path. You must get the road map to ensure safety of purpose. Read men, read books, ask questions, brainstorm, have a mastermind and chart out the road map to your destination. There is a way that leads to the place.

4. Have the weather picture in mind

When you are journeying on a rocky plain your preparation is different from when you are journeying by sea. To journey during winter, your equipment is different from when you journey during summer. Not foreseeing the challenges that need to be dealt with on your way leads you to be taken by surprise when you journey on the path of productivity. A proper weather forecast will help your preparation which is a step away from your destination.

The laws of life will terminate the struggles in life

By applying the principle of strategy you are bound to end up in prosperity. Begin with what you have and where you are. Plan with your available resources. Have operational targets, not vague aspirations; don't be abstract and unrealistic in your planning. Be concrete. Evolve step by step actions and watch your life propel towards your destination. If you do not want to agonise tomorrow: strategise today.

CHAPTER SIX:

SEVEN POWER POINTS TO PROSPERITY

Circle of power (2)

As you journey deeper into my circle of power, get ready to experience more power to move you up the ladder of productivity. Many struggle, many put in so much effort with little or no result. It is the picture of working like an elephant and eating like an ant. Some are tired, frustrated and have even lost hope, some have accepted a substandard level of living. Coping mechanisms are the order of the day. Dreams have been buried because circumstances seem to be difficult making things seem impossible. I challenge you at this point to believe with me that all things are possible. I present a technology that will take the

We should import more technology than finished products

sweat off your face and put a smile in its place. It will sharpen your skill and enhance your productivity. I am not saying that you don't have to work; you just need to know better ways to work. 'The how's' of life will always terminate the struggles in life. Get ready for more fuel to be powered to your next level.

1) Powered by Technology
2) Powered by Velocity
3) Powered by Density
4) Powered by Energy
5) Powered by Synergy
6) Powered by Opportunity
7) Powered by Integrity.

1. Powered By Technology

The British economist John Maynard Keynes pondered the dire circumstance of the great depression. From the depths of despair around him, he wrote in 1930 of the economic possibilities of future generations. At a time of distress and suffering, he envisaged the end of poverty in Great Britain and other industrialised countries. Toward the end of the twentieth century, Keynes emphasised the dramatic march of science and technology and the abilities of advances in technology to underpin continued economic growth at compound interest. I cannot but say that Keynes was more than correct in his predictions. Technology has always improved productivity which is the answer to poverty.

The results a farmer gets using orthodox equipment such as cutlasses and hoes cannot be compared to the effectiveness of farm operations powered by planters, tractors, and combine harvesters. The same applies to all aspects of life. Technology has literally turned the world right side up. I wonder what the world was like without planes, computers, communication gadgets in the media and so on. Technology has defeated gravity, it has defeated distance and it has even defeated poverty. Every country that has gone "TECHNOLOGICAL" has literally gone tops. Third World countries must begin to empower their people to read technology, think technology and ink technology. It will make all the difference in the scheme of things. It is interesting to know that countries that are first world today have all gone through periods of great depression. Things were not always the way they are today. If technology brought them out, it will bring us out. Our educative system must be structured in such a way that it properly prepares people to function in this area. While we try to develop in technology, we could start by importing more technology instead of just importing finished products.

Technology will add quality and quantity to your activity

Diffusion of technology

An Indian company had a remarkable arrangement with a hospital in Chicago, where doctors dictate their charts and transmit them by satellite to India as voice files at the end of each working day in Chicago. Because of the ten and half hour difference in time, the end of each working day in Chicago is the beginning of another in Chennai. When the voice files are received, dozens of young women who have taken special courses in medical data transcription sit in front of computer screens with headphones in place and speedily type in the medical charts of patients almost ten thousand miles away. They earn between $250 to $500 a month, depending on their particular level. It is between a tenth and a third of what a medical data transcriber might earn in the United States but this little diffusion has enhanced the productivity of many women by helping them earn enough money to make ends meet and live a decent life.

In Nigeria for instance, in the year 2001, President Olusegun Obasanjo adopted the technology of mobile phones. It made business transactions much easier. They could be carried out from virtually anywhere and at anytime. Virtually every Nigerian now has a phone and I can categorically say that it has enhanced productivity. Many people have learnt how to fix and repair phones; others buy and sell. It is now a multi-billion business in the country.

A Typical Example

Peak milk which is probably the biggest dairy provider in Nigeria, has its products in large tins. This cannot be afforded, regularly, by a large proportion of the population because of the pandemic of poverty. Another thing about the packaging was that, it was done in such a way that you couldn't buy a small quantity. If you just wanted a cup or two of tea, you had to buy the whole tin. I believe these are some of the thoughts that went into the young man's head who presented the idea of having peak milk (powdered) in sachets that would be small, affordable and could be used instantly for those who just want a cup or two of tea. This idea however was initially rejected. The young man took his idea to cowbell, another milk providing company; it was accepted and it was indeed an instant success. Cowbell became so popular and was highly patronised because of this simple technology. The young man would have made his millions, simply because of mental productivity. Today the same peak milk and many other beverage producers have employed this same technology and it has indeed been a blessing to Nigeria.

The practice of technology, increases man's capacity for productivity

Companies like MTN, Globacom, V-mobile, MTEL, are all a result of an explosion in the telecommunication industry. They have invested billions of naira into the Nigerian economy. Many people have found employment and have become productive; they have been empowered to climb the ladder of prosperity. Nitel; the government—owned telecommunications provider, even while operating as a virtual monopoly since its founding in 1962 (as Nigerian External Telecommunications NET) starved Nigerians of telecommunications services achieving only about 400,000 connected fixed lines for a population of over 100 million people.

If you want to avoid financial torment, get current

MTN already has over twenty-five million phone lines. Without any fear of contradiction, technology is indeed a boost both to productivity and prosperity.

Technology however, does not have to always mean high—tech machinery and equipment. It could apply in areas of management skills, human relations and business. It could cover the small and big, simple and complex. The point is there is a better way to do what you are doing. Mental work will always be superior to physical work. It yields more dividends, it yields more results. To be involved in technology, you must appreciate brain work.

A report from the 25th FAO regional conference for Asia and the pacific in Yokohama, Japan on the 28th August to 1st September, 2000 also emphasised the need for developing a society driven by technology. Technology has been the cornerstone of progress in agricultural production, particularly with the growing scarcity of cultivable land and increasing populations. It was harnessed to improve the productivity in rice, maize, sugar cane and oil crops. New technology in post-harvest handling and processing of palm oil, cocoa beans and natural rubber were also developed and widely adopted. In some other countries, rural electrification played an important role in enhancing agricultural productivity. While biotechnology is yet to be fully harnessed in the region, some applications can already be seen in the alteration of plants, animals and microbes. Technology has always enhanced productivity. Your case and that of your country cannot be different, get updated, get current or you will be left behind. Appreciate technology, get involved in technology and see your life move to the next level.

2. Powered By Velocity

You will remain low if you are slow

As a business man you must be able to beat time and distance, you must create a mechanism by which orders can be made on the goods and services you offer. It will always enhance customer satisfaction and confidence. With such services you are already productive. Patronage will increase, leading to more money coming into your venture. Jimoh Ibrahim, the business magnate, once said that in business, the fast eats up the slow.

This concept remains valuable even in the context of decision making and carrying out plans. Yes, it is important to plan and prepare but this should not take eternity. You will remain low if you are slow. Every man needs a level of speed to make it in life. Bill Gates was once asked, how he made it so fast? He said they (Bill & Paul) were scared, someone else would get there before them. No matter how unique your concept is you must understand others could be thinking along the same lines. Velocity will give you competitive advantage. Stop procrastinating and start acting; your services and goods could well be the solutions to someone else's problem.

It doesn't make sense, launching out, without first being dense

3. Powered By Density

Think of your market as a pool of fish or a herd of animals. Does your market contain enough animals? Is it a growing or declining market? Is it easy to find where they are and what their feeding pattern is? Are they really hungry? Is the weather condition ideal for a hunting expedition? Is there a certain bait that sends your market to a feeding frenzy? Are they willing to come out of the safe, dark depths of the bottom to fight for this new bait? Can you catch them? Getting the right answers to these questions will put you on the right track. One of the researches you must carry out before venturing into any business is the size of your market. You must find out how much people want the product you are offering. There is no point in going through the stress of making goods and services no one would want to buy. The relevance of your products to humanity will give you the cutting edge. You will always have millions of people patronising your business.

Bill Gates is the wealthiest man today because the magnitude of his market is virtually the whole world. Find out the problems of humanity, look within yourself to see the talents and abilities, if you solve those problems you are on your way to the top.

Sometime ago, I was studying the world markets to know what was happening so that I could properly position myself for relevance and riches. I was tracing where the wealth of the world was going so I could get my own chunk. I made ample discoveries. I stumbled on the MDGs (Millennium Development Goals) set by the UN member nations. It contained eight different areas of existence that needed to be settled in Third World countries. I didn't have to look very far, the first goal was it; it dawned on me like a ray of light, what was this goal? It was the eradication of extreme hunger and poverty. It perfectly matched my passion and gifts.

Make sure the size of your supply can meet the size of demand; at least to a great extent

Even when disseminating information, I always talk about eradicating poverty. That is the crux of my talks and writings. I emphasise productivity as the answer to poverty. Even before stumbling on the MDGs, somehow I always used to say that I don't intend to die leaving Africa as a Third World continent. Everything seemed to match. I found a relevant need that had a large market. Imagine all the Third World countries and Third World people. Even certain people living in first world countries, including those who are citizens still have a productivity and poverty problem. I had found my path in life. A lifelong journey had begun; I began to develop myself along those lines. When I started calling myself a National Reformer, many wondered what it was, but I knew one thing: I had found a path to connect with my passion. This book is one of the results of this discovery. Imagine how many people in the world this book is relevant to, study the markets, find problems, look within your passion and find the connection.

The moment you find this connection, you are ready for production.

After settling the issue of the size of your market, you must be aware of the size of your solution. If you are going to be disseminating

Concentration is the mother of distinction

information, you must stock yourself with enough matter in order to deliver to those who need your information. You cannot afford to be shallow. You must read, study, and think beyond the average man. Whichever area you want to embark on you must be replete with information. Then be well-stocked with supply. It would be foolish for me to only print a thousand copies of this book when we have over 140 Third World countries numbering billions of people. Get velocity, get density and you will be sure to have productivity. My physics teacher taught me that mass or density multiplied by velocity will give you momentum. Get ready to move at a pace that will shock you and those around you. When people come to look for you where you have always been, they will be surprised to see how far and fast you have moved. Remember it doesn't take struggles, it takes steps.

4. Powered By Energy

The world today is filled with many opportunities to be seized. Some areas have been exploited more than others. The existence of many market options sometimes leaves people confused, not knowing exactly where to focus their time and energy. Some are attracted to certain markets because several individuals have laboured there to make these areas very desirable even though they were not originally suitable markets. People no longer concentrate;

they are distracted by what others have done and are doing. Little do they know that they can work at what they are doing in a particular area until they become cities set on hills that cannot be hidden.

Stop dying in isolation, get connected and you will be elevated

It is important to understand the concept of diversification and functional specialisation as it relates to your productivity. To diversify is to spread your resources to many business areas and options. This helps you develop multiple streams of income which is a path to real wealth. However, as important as diversification is, timing can have a huge impact. When starting out to make a particular product or service available, I always prescribe to individuals and organisations to specialise first. It is easier to make progress when you are known for something and not for everything. We should not be jacks of all trades and masters of none. Productivity is more likely in the presence of speciality and not generality. We have too many general contractors in Africa that is why the number of inventions are low. Our creative energies are so spread in a manner that we do not give the required time to what we are doing to get the best out of them. However, once you have discovered and developed your speciality, it is advisable to begin to spread your energies to other areas you are wired for to increase your income flow and have escape routes to help recover from any business recessions that may occur.

The energy we are referring to here is that of focus and concentration. When you stay on your course, you will not miss your cause.

If you don't learn to mingle with the right people you are liable to fumble

Concentration is the pathway to distinction. Begin to focus your talents and time on one area of your life and business at a time per season, and in no time it will improve and develop a beauty and attractiveness that will announce you to your world.

5. Powered By Synergy

When you see geese heading south for the winter flying along in a V formation, it might interest you to know that science has discovered why they fly that way. Research has revealed that as each bird flaps its wings, it creates uplift for the bird immediately behind it. By flying in a V formation the whole flock adds at least 71 percent greater flying range than if each bird flew on its own. Whenever a goose falls out of formation, it suddenly feels the drag and resistance of trying to do it alone. It quickly gets back into the formation to take advantage of the lifting power of the bird immediately in front. When the lead goose gets tired he rotates back in the V and another goose flies at the point. The geese honk from behind to encourage those up front to keep their speed. When a goose gets sick, or it is wounded by gunfire and falls out, two other geese fall out of formation and follow it down to help and protect it. They stay with the goose until it is either able to fly again or it dies and then they launch out.

In the pursuit of eradicating poverty no one can achieve it alone; you will need to mingle with other people. Countries will have to relate with other countries, organisations will have to mobilise their human resources to accomplish their ultimate goals. You cannot isolate yourself; you need the input of others. This

Your capacity for productivity, needs the window called opportunity, for it to yield prosperity

book is a product of synergy. At this point I have read hundreds of books and articles that have sharpened my synthesis process and served as a pool of information and inspiration to draw from. Stop dying in isolation. Get connected and you will be elevated.

6. Powered By Opportunity

I remember vividly one evening—I was in my final year in university—I stood at a particular angle looking at thousands of people celebrating, moving from place to place. It was a very rowdy day. I had been in that school for five years at the time and had never seen such a crowd of people. This school, which was quite sparsely populated when I came in had suddenly become densely populated. That evening was the matriculation day for fresh incoming students. As I stood there alone, I was isolated from the celebrations. I wondered how many problems this mass of people had that needed to be solved. In the midst of everything I saw an opportunity. Anywhere you have people; you have the opportunity to sell goods or services.

For any product or service, your market is mostly people. I called a friend and told him that the school was ripe for harvest. Three months later I packaged a two day programme that attracted close to 4 thousand attendants. Wow!!! Success you may say. Many saw that same crowd but I saw a crowd with problems, I had the answer. You must turn on your radar as you read the papers, watch television and walk on the streets. If you look hard enough, you will find something. Opportunities are all around us; your capacity for productivity needs the window called opportunity for it to yield prosperity. Be an opportunity hunter. Instead of complaining, look out for a need you can meet and meet that need.

I once read of two American college students who went for a holiday trip in India. They noticed so many people were not wearing shoes, one of the boys mocked at such poverty, the other saw an opportunity. He saw a shoe empire. He then tried out an idea when he got back to America. He ordered some cheap plastic sandals and took them to India. It worked like magic and, in no time he was importing millions of sandals into India. He instantly became a millionaire. One saw a problem, the other saw an opportunity. Change your perception of the things that happen around you be a solution thinker to problems, and you will begin to notice gold mines in the same places you used to walk by. You too can become a millionaire by finding an opportunity to release your productivity.

7. Powered By Integrity

I know integrity is not usually a popular topic these days. I remember reading Stephen Covey's book "The 7 Habits of Highly Effective People". He spoke about a discovery he'd made when studying

Integrity is what you connect to keep opportunity open

for his doctorate. He said books that were written about 100 years ago emphasised character ethics beyond personality ethics as a basis for success. He went on to state that the trend began to change as the years passed by. The emphasis seemed to shift from character ethics to personality ethics. This is an anomaly that this generation must face and correct. It is responsible for the kind of corruption and mess in our societies today. People are willing to make it at all cost notwithstanding the methods. We have people with charisma today who can open doors but it is totally a different ball game to stay successful. Success exposes one to many temptations and challenges that only character can handle. If you don't want your prosperity to be a flash in the pan, if you want true and lasting prosperity, you must begin to develop and practice integrity. You must develop truth, honesty, sincerity, transparency and many other ingredients that breed integrity. You don't have to join the crowd, single yourself out by integrity, it always pays.

I remember a story a senior pharmacist friend once told me about his business. He needed an additional sum of $150,000 for a particular business transaction. He then met a certain lady friend who had quite a rich nice husband. The husband was a little skeptical but still gave the money. This was because the wife had quite a good character reports to tell about the pharmacist. After he carried out the business transaction, he returned the money on schedule as promised, even before he was asked to. The husband of the wife was impressed with this extreme display of integrity. He then told the pharmacist he would like to invest another one million dollars into the business which he did. Imagine what would have happened if he didn't live up to his side of the bargain. His capacity opened a door and his integrity kept the door open. Just as opportunity is that which connects you to your capacity for productivity, integrity is what you connect to opportunity to keep it open. As you exude integrity, you will suddenly notice peoples' trust in you grow and want to be part of what you're doing. Your life and business then receives more energy for productivity.

Trust in a relationship is like "the power of thrust": It will take you forward

CHAPTER SEVEN:

SIX POWER ROUTES TO PROSPERITY

The concept of power in our lives cannot be overemphasised as it is critical for conquest, and vital for victory. The more

Power is critical for conquest, vital for victory

power you have the more energy you have. The more energy you have, the more productive you become. Power helps you to push beyond the necessary responsibility to attain productivity as it will help you cross the hurdles and climb the mountains. It is needed to prevail, it is needed for progress. Stop living a powerless life, plug into my circles of power and watch energy surge through your life helping you become that dream person you have always imagined.

Circle of Power (3)

1) Powered by Literacy
2) Powered by Salary
3) Powered by Royalty
4) Powered by Industry
5) Powered by Frugality
6) Powered by Importunity

1. Powered By Literacy

During the gold-rush days in the United States, an uncle of the famous RU Darby was caught by the gold rush with his burning desire for gold, and the prospects that lay ahead; he decided to go hunting. He staked a claim and went to work with a pick and shovel. The venture was tough but his desire for gold was definite.

After weeks of hard labour, he was rewarded by the discovery of the shining ore. He needed machinery to bring the ore to the surface. Quietly, he covered up the mine and retraced all his footsteps to his homeland around Williamsburg, Maryland and told his relatives and neighborurs of the strike. Full of enthusiasm and hope, they got the money together for the needed machinery and had it shipped. Darby and his uncle went back to work the mine.

The first cart of ore was mined, and shipped to a smelting plant. The returns proved they had one of the richest mines in Colorado. A few more carts of that ore would clear their debts, then would come mouth watering profits.

Down went the drills! Up went the hopes of Darby and his uncle. Then something happened, the vein of the gold disappeared. They had come to the *Literacy prepares you for activity, empowers you for productivity, secures your prosperity and establishes your destiny* end of the rainbow, and the pot of gold was no longer there. Drilling on desperately they tried to pick up the trail again but to no avail. Finally they decided to throw in the towel.

They sold the machinery to a junk man for a few hundred dollars, and took the next train back home. Some junk men may be stupid, but not this one. He turned the magical key Darby and his uncle hadn't. That simple key made a yawning gap of difference in their lives. This junk man ended up going home with millions of dollars in ore from the mine. The same piece of land Darby and his uncle ventured into was the same one the junk man ventured into. This one key I am putting in your hand is so simple but could make a million dollars for you in no time.

What was so different about this junk man? He called a mining engineer to look at the mine and do a little calculation. The engineer advised that the project had failed because the owners were not familiar with the fault lines. His calculation showed that the vein would be just found three feet from where Darby had stopped drilling and so it was. Imagine what Darby missed.

You must take advantage of the power of literacy: your ability to read and write. You must be able to read the circumstances of whatever venture you are into. You must be informed and literate enough about what it will take, if you don't want to waste time and energy. Where you cannot read between the lines, hire some expertise; remember it could be worth a million dollars.

2. Powered By Salary

One of the major postulations today is that true development can only come when people stop the 'employee rush' to become employers of labour. Many a time, it is said a salary is not enough to make you a millionaire; it is often referred to as a slow way up the line. Many from the older generation who are salary earners do not help matters;

their inability to manage and multiply their salary earnings leaves them particularly broke and complaining. This has left many young people with unbalanced philosophies, worn out as entrepreneurs going through hardships that could be avoided by more informed decisions. I strongly believe in living beyond a salary. I have always had the employer-of—labour mentality. Nevertheless that does not negate the power of a salary. It is not a bad place to start from. Many people have tried to go somewhere from nowhere, rather than going somewhere from some place.

Your salary is a seed, don't eat it all up

Getting involved in a business either as a passive or active partner can take as much as three years to begin to yield some tangible results. Sometimes less, sometimes more. The period it takes for a business to germinate is usually a trying one; many people cannot make ends meet. Some people begin to beg, some are discouraged by their challenges and begin to steal and lie for a few pennies. With a more intelligent plan, this could be avoided. Even when your business begins to germinate there are things you might need, some extra source of funds or something to leverage the level of risk in your business.

Having a good salary from a job could serve as capital for whatever business you want to do. Instead of becoming a perpetual borrower, you could reduce your expenditure and leaks, you could save more till you have a good amount to kick off with. Don't be afraid to start small, for every forest has its root in a seed. With some effort and diligence, your business could grow into an empire. If you have not gone beyond a salary, especially if you are not wired totally for entrepreneurship, go and get yourself a job.

I remember struggling to put a little seminar together that cost just a couple of thousands. At the time it was quite difficult to get investors to invest in my seminars. This particular experience actually set me thinking. I had some qualifications that could earn me a paid job of about that same amount at least, but I was also in the 'entrepreneur craze'.

Think big, start small As an entrepreneur I would not dare play down what I do, but too many move with half truth and get into trouble. Had I a salary I could save monthly for my seminars and do a seminar once in three months before the seminars grow to a point where it attracts sponsorship and helpers. Making enough funds from profits and then have more frequent seminars. Develop your plan wisely, count the cost and then launch out. There is dignity in labour.

3. Powered By Royalty

Reading Robert G Allen, the author of "Nothing Down" he states that in about the 1980's when he started writing, even teenagers working in McDonalds were earning more than he was. He put in over 1,000 hours of work into the book. He was not looking for a salary, he wanted royalties. It took about two years for the money to start rolling in. Today, millions and millions of dollars have come in from that effort.

As good as a salary is, there is something better, it is called royalties. I have personally made up my mind that I am going to leave at least 100 books for my world to benefit from my wealth of knowledge. As I write this, I already have the concept for eight others. Imagine the impact and influence this will have in the lives of millions all over the world.

My journey to financial intelligence did not consciously begin until I came close to finishing university. I went to Lagos state to obtain a visa to travel to London. I ended up staying a few months with a senior sister of mine who was a banker. The thing I liked about her was that, she valued and knew how to control her money. A multiplier, oh yes she was. She was earning a salary but it was obvious she was living beyond her salary. Prying a little, I discovered she was actively involved in the stock market, and had millions in stocks. I learnt a lot from her; she gave me books such as Think and Grow Rich, Rich Dad poor Dad, The Richest Man in Babylon and so many others that broadened my horizon. You too can begin to journey on this same path. When you are on a salary, your pay cheque stops the day you stop working. You are paid once for many hours of work, but when you are on royalties, you are paid many times spanning over years for the same effort. At this level, your money and time naturally brings in money. I recently saw a new edition of "Think and Grow Rich" celebrating 15 million copies sold in 65 years. Can you beat that? It probably took close to twelve 12 months of active writing, which has led to a stream of income for 65 years and beyond. Begin to grow from salary to royalty that is where the money is.

4. Powered By Frugality

Billionaire, John D Rockefeller taught his children always to value money. He paid each of his five sons an allowance of 25 cents a week and they had to earn the rest of the money they got. To earn part of that extra money, one of his sons Nelson had to raise vegetables and rabbits. According to Nelson, they always worked. All the boys were required to keep daily account books. They were required to save ten percent of their income and give away ten percent to charity and account for the rest. They had to balance their account books every month and be able to explain what happened to every penny they earned. Nelson went on to serve as Governor of the State of New York for many years and ultimately became the Vice President of the United States. One of his brothers, David, became the Chairman of Chase Manhattan Bank. He said: "We all profited by the experience, especially when it came to the experience of valuing money."

Frugality refers to being careful about your expenditure, being economical. This is a character trait you find amongst wealthy people. To accumulate wealth in the long run, you need to pour money into investments. To get this capital, you will many times have to deny yourself of legitimate needs which are not too necessary for now. The craze for flamboyance is the bane of many people. They use investment capital for personal uses; profits that are meant to be reinvested into the business are used to buy cars or for trips abroad. With proper planning and hard work, all these are bound to come but the timing must be right. The ability to manage your cash flow will determine if you will be rich or poor. Do not allow the desire for instant gratification to steal a glorious future from you. The billionaire Rockefeller could have lavished dollars on his children but he knew financial skill was more important than finance itself and that is what he gave his children. The rest is history.

> The inability to manage cash flow,
> is the reason for much damage

A wise man once said, save your money, and then spend the rest. Don't spend your money and then save the rest. This will make a whole lot of difference in your world of finances. You cannot escape frugality if you want productivity and prosperity. Begin to examine your expenses at the end of each month. You don't need to be an accountant to do that. Have it all written down. With this you can study your spending patterns. You will be able to identify where excesses are and subsequently curtail your spending. You must look for leaks and plumb them so that you have enough money at your disposal for investments. Do not sacrifice your tomorrow on the alter of today. Stop thinking short term and start thinking long term. It is the style of the wealthy.

5. Powered By Industry

While I was at university, my course required that I work for a whole year before my finals as part of my academic training for a university degree. It is called industrial training. I was still in my very early twenties at the time. I believed age was quite on my side so I decided that this year would be an experimenting time for me. It was one of those years that led to more self discoveries. It was also a year that gave birth to many passions that still drive me today.

I decided in that one year, to work in as many places as possible. I wanted to know the particular environments that I could consider to work in after school. I ended up working in the Ministry of Defence and Ministry of Agriculture. Before the end of the one year experience, the entrepreneur inside me had taken a hold of me. I left the public sector and started a little poultry farm to get some experience as an agricultural economist in training. I discovered within this time why the Nigerian Civil Service was as unproductive as it was. That period was a gestation period for my desire to see the extreme lack of productivity eradicated from my country. I am told that a civil servant in Japan is required to put in 12 hours of active service every day into work. Little wonder that Japan is a world power today. I met a very placid and lackadaisical attitude in the public sector. People could just walk in and out of their offices at any time. However the private sector was more disciplined and effective. Working hours were usually from 8am—4pm with an hour for lunch. On Fridays work usually came to a close at about 2pm. This was the pattern of those on the lower scale, no wonder many of them stayed there so long and never had enough money. Compare this to mighty Japan. The seven hours for work was eaten up by phone calls and gossip. Many even slept at work because they were idle. If change is to come to Third World people and countries, our attitude to work must change. We must begin to love work and put in many productive hours to eradicate poverty. Many a time I was even told to go home by senior colleagues in the middle of a working day because there was nothing to do. Can you imagine that? The only place success comes before work is in the dictionary. I found out early in life that I must be willing to put in an average of fifteen hours of productive effort working, five to six days a week if I wanted to be among the top ten percent in my industry. Don't get scared, don't give excuses; everyone will eventually lie on their bed the way they make it. If you love what you do, hard work will not be a problem. Get busy and stop being silly. Nothing comes easily.

A life-changing discovery for me came when I was told that what work was to an adult, play was to children. Children cannot be healthy without playing. Can you remember when you were one? They are naturally wired and tailored by God at that level to love jumping around. This actually made me more accommodating to my many nephews who were always jumping around the house at the time. The implication of this is that your life and business needs work to stay healthy and productive. Stop killing the potential you carry by not doing anything. Attention is food for any vision. You have stared at it long enough, start feeding it, and it will soon start growing.

Get busy and stop being silly, nothing comes easily

- Employ your talents
- Employ your time
- Employ your resources

Do these at all times, value them, control them, multiply and share them and you are bound to be an industrious man. Industry always commands productivity.

Attention is the food for any vision, feed it and it will grow. Starve it and it will die.

6. Powered By Importunity

Years ago in Philistine, there was a great famine that came over the land. It reduced agricultural activities to a minimum. Farmers could hardly raise enough food for themselves, let alone for the general population. There was however a special Israeli farmer who got over hundred fold return that same year. He became so large in animal and crop farming that he was feared and asked to go to a land away from theirs. His success had attracted some envy among the citizens of the country.

When he moved to a valley nearby, he began to reopen the wells which his father had dug. The local shepherds in this new plain turned against him and closed up the wells. They argued with him saying, this is our water. Having named the place argument, he moved and dug again finding water which attracted more fights. The Israeli farmer moved again with his men still digging for water. The local shepherds finally left him alone. He then called the name of the well 'room enough' because he believed God.

Continuity + Intensity = Importunity

Let's be realistic, no technology or philosophy is a magic formula. No seminar that is realistic will give you information that could just turn things around in the twinkle of an eye. Everything you do requires time and effort. The germination time of your dreams is usually the most trying time. Many give up at this stage. You must activate the ability to sustain your steam, you must keep doing what you are doing until you get the required results.

Think of all the great people: Abraham Lincoln, Nelson Mandela and many others you know and admire today. It took them some time to get there. Be sure you are on the right track; be sure your plot is right and you are sure to arrive.

Developing importunity

1) Keep your vision in view
2) Look at others who made it through
3) Constantly encourage yourself
4) Give your ears only to positive talk
5) Constant praying
6) Spiritual food

Some make it while in their teens, some in their twenties, some in their sixties and even seventies. Whichever age bracket you fall into, it is not too early neither is it too late pick up your boots and begin to run, continuity and intensity will give you importunity.

THE COMPLETE PICTURE

Circle of power (1)

1) Powered by Mentality
2) Powered by Strategy

Circle of power (2)

1) Powered by Technology
2) Powered by Velocity
3) Powered by Density
4) Powered by Energy
5) Powered by Synergy
6) Powered by Opportunity
7) Powered by Integrity

Circle of Power (3)

1) Powered by Literacy
2) Powered by Salary
3) Powered by Royalty
4) Powered by Frugality
5) Powered by Industry
6) Powered by Importunity.

PART THREE

LEADERSHIP AND CHANGE

'Leadership that cannot bring about change
should be changed'

CHAPTER EIGHT:

LEADERSHIP IN CONTEXT

The word leadership is not an unfamiliar word to many. Nevertheless, the understanding of this ten letter word means ten different things to ten different people. Geoff Rutter once said "Leadership is the most observed yet least understood concept in the world." The concept of leadership cannot be overemphasised as it controls our lives, homes, organisations and countries. It is simply rational that anything that determines progress and productivity should be studied, understood and eventually mastered. The understanding of this concept will help you to:

1) Know how and who to elect or appoint into leadership positions in your particular environment.
2) Know if you, as a person have developed your leadership potentials.
3) Know who to follow.
4) Increase your present level of performance.

You are about to discover the difference between success and failure, happiness and sadness, riches and rags. I am about to unfold why every individual, family, country and organisation is where it is today. This piece of information will catapult you to your next level. Third World countries and Third World people will remain where they are until this concept is understood and applied. It has enough power to get anyone and any country into a first world situation.

Leaders vs Leadership

The inability to differentiate between these two words is one of the reasons why the Third World is where it is

The right identity is vital to understand your responsibility

today. Before any individual can give proper leadership, he must first develop the leader within, as your outer life cannot be better than your inner life. You must first focus on developing the leader inherent in you to a point where he is strong enough to assert real leadership. It is therefore paramount to know the difference between these two words. Let us look at some definitions from experts, to help boost your understanding.

- Dr M John: A leader is a man who knows the road, can keep ahead and pull others after him.

- President Harry Truman: The ability to get others to do what they don't want to do, what they are too lazy to do, and like it.

- Dr Chung: There are only three kinds of people in the world, those who are immovable, movable and those who move them both.

- Napoleon: There are no bad soldiers only bad officers. The general is the army.

- Harish Shukla: A leader is one who can get the job done from followers without force.

- John Maxwell again says: Leadership is influence—nothing more, nothing less.

- Warren Bennis: Leadership is the capacity to translate vision into reality.

Misconceptions of a Leader

1) The man with the money
2) The man with position
3) The man with fame

The leader comes before his leadership. One of the problems in Third World countries is that there are people in charge who are not yet leaders, so their leadership is not effective. This table below will help differentiate the two words.

Leader	Leadership
Who you are	What you do
Being	Doing
Passive	Active
Personality	Activity
Internal	External

The leader is the man who communicates, inspires, motivates, moves and acts. In my search to understand who a leader is and the concept of leadership, I have studied many definitions and viewpoints on these words. I decided to look up the Greek use of this word from which the English language sprang amongst other languages;

it presents metaphorical and literal expressions of the concept.

A) Phero meaning a gate

B) Anago meaning a ladder

Others are to Train and to Drive which are metaphorical presentations. From these we can now say:

1) Leadership is making contact and connecting to people, inspiring them towards a common goal (TRAIN).
2) Leadership is helping others step up in life not minding being stepped on in the process (LADDER).
3) Leadership is providing an entry for others into more favourable conditions of life (GATE).
4) Leadership is connecting with people to the point where you are followed (TRAIN).
5) Leadership is providing direction and motion towards a particular destination. It is knowing where to head and being in control through the journey (DRIVER).

Let's look at a couple of literal definitions of leadership in the Greek language:

A) Ago meaning to carry or bear

B) Exago meaning to lead out

From these I further present other definitions of leadership:

6) Leadership is helping to reduce the responsibility for the destiny of others. It is serving as an instrument and

not as the ultimate means to the accomplishment of a task.

7) Leadership is enabling an exit from unfavourable conditions in life.

In conclusion before we try to demonstrate leadership we must first build the leader inside us, as leadership is only the ripple-effect of a leader. He may not be the man with the position but he is the man with the function.

To develop the leader, first we simply need to change how and what we think as our thought patterns determine our behavioural patterns. To be a leader you must first think like a leader. Let's take a look at a few thought patterns.

1) See a need and take the lead
2) Be an initiator and a motivator
3) What can I give not what can I get
4) Others before myself
5) We and not I
6) How can I make my world better and bigger?

Every theology produces a particular psychology and your psychology determines your activity

These thought patterns will produce behavioural patterns that will make a leader of any follower. Make the choice today, to live like a leader. Any life with vision, direction and passion will always increase in performance and productivity. Bring a new level of leadership to your life, organisation and country and watch relevance and riches come into your life.

CHAPTER NINE:

THE CHARACTER OF TRUE LEADERSHIP

Day in day out millions of people come out of various leadership crucibles, expected to have gone through various developmental processes, coming out as diamond leaders who will pioneer change in their organisations and countries. Some are leaders over a few, some are leaders over many. Your leadership may be governmental, spiritual, family clan or it may just be over yourself; however wide the sphere of our leadership, we are all meant to be leaders in certain areas at certain points in our lives.

You will need character
if you are going to matter

The misconception about the character of leadership has led to many 'factory rejects'. So many people develop in the wrong direction. Their formation is faulty so it affects their ability to provide leadership that brings about change. All change that has ever occurred at all levels of life always begins with one man; you could be the very next. The decay that has eaten deep into our societies has made the topic of character very unattractive. You are even called names when you stand for justice and truth in our present day and time. It is in the light of this that I write this chapter. Character and change are two things that go hand in hand. You cannot take one in isolation. The older generations of leaders unfortunately have not provided steps towards true integrity for the younger generation to follow. That is why we are in the mess we are in. One of our projects is called project SAG: Save A Generation. We hold seminars that emphasise character development, we redefine words such as success, wealth, and influence so that our young people have a proper grip of what these words truly mean and how to achieve these qualities rather than abusing sound moral principles. I will not be able to address the whole issue of character development, in this book, but I will however provide a foundation you can build on. The leader is not the one with fame, money or position, he is the one with function, the one who possesses the true essence of a leader, the one with character. I will be addressing character in three dimensions.

- Loving
- Modeling and
- Serving.

1. Loving

In the 1960s, the brother to the Vice President of the Philippines was a very wealthy businessman. By today's standards his asset base was said to be well over $1 billion dollars. Mr. Lopez had interests that included many media stations, newspapers, radio, a large utility company and many others.

Love is the oxygen of life, to live and not to love is not to live at all

In 1972, Ferdinand Marcos declared martial law in the Philippines. He seized more than mere power. He seized all media outlets, newspapers, alongside many other assets; he also went further and nationalised them. In doing so, he kidnapped the president of one of the television stations who happened to be the son of Mr. Lopez who was at that time in America. He was given a call and told to relinquish rights over all properties or have his son killed. Do you know

Three great forces are faith, hope and love but the greatest of all is love

what he did? If you were in the same shoes what choice would you make? How this man acquired his massive business empire I really don't know but he lost everything because he loved his son enough to make that sacrifice. You might say he made that choice because it was his son in question. However it does express that man can do anything to make another better in the presence of love. If he had loved his country just a little compared to how he loved his son, I'm sure he would have been a more caring and effective leader. The emergence of leaders who will be motivated by this force called love will be the turning point of any country as it carries within it sacrifice, endurance, compassion, passion and many other necessary traits a leader needs to pioneer and cause change.

Almost 1,500 years BC there was a great fight between Moab and Israel. Israel pressed hard against the Moabites with great intensity. The King of Moab seeing that the battle was almost lost took a special squad of 700 swordsmen; however this could not get them victory. The King at this point was desperate, scared and confused. Many of his fighters had been slain. Was he going to loose his kingdom to Israel? Was he going to be captured as a spoil of war? Moved with compassion to save his people from destruction, he took his eldest son who was to take over from him as King and slew as a sacrifice to the gods. This very act of bravery inspired by the love for his country beyond the love for self, led to a great indignation falling upon Israel. What would you have done? This act saved the people of Moab that day. This may sound like a myth to you; but I dare say that any organisation or country that has a leader like the King of Moab is already in for true and lasting change. In the presence of love, nothing is too much to do for the benefit of another. Love always reaches out. It considers others, and is not selfish in actions. We need leaders so much today who do not just love power, influence and money but have a truly loving heart for the people they govern.

In my opinion love is the oxygen of man, to live and not to love is not to live at all.

- Love God
- Love your work
- Love people and
- Love yourself

2. Serving

Have you ever been so hungry and couldn't wait to cook? You then rushed to a restaurant with the anticipation of having your hunger satisfied. However you got very impatient as your order was not served at the pace you had expected. Disturbed by your hunger pangs you went to the counter to lay your complaint. To your greatest surprise, you were told the food couldn't be served because food wasn't ready. The manager explained to you about an operational challenge they had been having throughout the day. You left disappointed with your hunger pangs unattended to. From discussions I have had with people, I have learnt that some people don't like the concept of service because of the way it has been presented to them. Some see service as being weak and foolish; it is perceived that you have to be at a low ebb to serve. The popular understanding of the word servant from which service is derived hasn't helped matters at all. Taking our cue from the story above, there are people with several needs in life, not necessarily hunger like our story above. Some need shelter, clothing, instruction or one of many other needs. The list is endless.

For every need, God has put into different people what it takes to meet those needs. What some call gifts, others call talents; some even call it potential.

The promise of your greatness lies in the key of service

Whatever name you prefer, the fact remains that a solution to a problem lies within you. Just as our hungry fellow expected food to have been cooked to satisfy his hunger so are many people waiting for you to cook your potential to the point that it could be 'served' to another, to meet a need. This is a simple concept of service. To date I am told the star of David remains on the flag of Israel. Over the waves of time, many have come and gone but I believe the way Saul of Tarsus summarised the life of David is the reason his star still remains in his honour. Thousands of Kings and thousands of years have not been able to erase his input to the country. Saul of Tarsus turned Paul puts it this way. David served his generation and slept . . . . The true way to greatness is service. Who will miss you when you are gone, what will you be remembered for? You cannot bless others and not be blessed; it is simply the law of sowing and reaping. Someone out there is starving because you have refused to do anything; men of service are agents of change. They are trail blazers and they make things happen wherever they are. The one who is great is the one who serves.

3. Modeling

A meeting was held in a court of public opinion on August 28th, 2004. The topic was on role models, heroes and leaders. The meeting was comprised of people from all walks of life. The basic character traits of honesty, compassion and hard work, among others, were spelt out for the proper selection of leaders.

90% disagreed that success is how much money a man can make

75% agreed that it is how others think of you

100% agreed that it is what a person does to help others

I have discovered that people who manifest a duplicity of personality are not able to switch on their productivity.

Any leader who cannot be a model cannot truly excel

Leadership deals with human relationships and relationships are built and sustained based on trust. Where there is no character, there can be no trust: where there is no trust, leadership cannot exist and where there is no leadership change is not in view. We must begin to tailor our development in the right direction.

Albert Schweitzer says "Example is not the main thing it is the only thing." The world today more than ever is in need of role models, people who will provide the true paths for others to follow. The scary thing is that in the absence of positive role models, people will follow negative role models.

We need leaders whose reputations resemble their character. Hypocrisy is not a good breeding ground for productive leadership. We need charismatic leaders yes, but we need more men of character. Any leader who cannot be a model is not likely to excel, he may have his position but not his leadership. Leadership is not what you can be appointed or voted into, true leadership is earned, and true leadership is that which attracts followers because they have seen in the leader a person they want to be like.

Leadership that is modeled is compelling, it has a strong magnetic pull, an aura that inspires and motivates people to journey on a particular course. Lee Iaccoca says that a leader should not demand of others what he cannot demand of himself. People are more inspired by what they see lived than what they hear said; it gives it substance and reality. How many leaders today end up in scandals of immorality, corruption and other evils that could have been avoided if character was in place? Leadership that will matter is leadership with character. The true character of leadership is loving, serving and modeling. Chinua Achebe a prolific Nigerian writer said that the challenge of Nigerian leaders is their refusal to

People who manifest a duplicity of personality cannot switch on their productivity

rise to the challenge of personal example which is the hallmark of true leadership.

An Inspiration

Mother Teresa was born in Agnes Gonxha Bojaxhiu in Skopje, Macedonia, on August 27th,1910. Her family was of Albanian descent. At the age of twelve, she felt the strong call of God. She knew she had to be a missionary to spread the love of Christ. At the age of eighteen, she left her parental home in Skopje and joined the sisters of Lareto, an Irish community of nuns with a mission in India. From 1931 to 1948 Mother Teresa taught at St Mary's High School in Calcutta, but the suffering and poverty she glimpsed outside the wall of the convent made such a deep impression on her that in 1948 she received permission from her superiors to leave the convent school to devote herself to working among the poorest of the poor in the slums of Calcutta. In the absence of funds, she was not deterred but depended on divine providence, and started an open-air school for slum children. Soon, she was joined by voluntary helpers, and financial support was also forthcoming.

This made it possible for her to extend her work. On October 7th, *Real Leaders are healers* 1950. Mother Teresa received permission from the Holy See to start her own order; The Missionaries of Charity, whose primary task was to love and care for those persons nobody was prepared to look after. Today, the order comprises active and contemplative branches of sisters and brothers in many countries. In 1963, both the contemplative branch of the sisters and active branch was formed. Many extensions have occurred over the years.

They provide effective help to the poorest of the poor in a number of countries in Asia, Africa and Latin America, and they undertake relief work in the wake of natural catastrophes such as floods, epidemics, famine and also assist refugees.

The order has assets in Europe, North America and Australia, where they take care of the housebound, alcoholics, the homeless and those living with AIDS. They have over one million co-workers in more than 40 countries.

Mother Teresa's work has been recognised and acclaimed throughout the world and during her lifetime, she received a number of awards and distinctions including the Pope John Paul (XXIII) peace prize for her promotion of international peace, 1971, Nehru prize for her promotion of international peace and understanding in 1972, Nobel peace prize in 1979, indigos height civilian award, presidential model for freedom in 1998, honorary citizen of war in 1996. She died on September 5th 1997.

Wow! I don't know about you but her life stimulates and inspires me. You can see the expression of love, service, and modelling in

If you don't develop in the right direction, you will not be able to bring about a revolution

the life of this woman. She was ready to sacrifice the comfort within the convent walls to reach those nobody was willing to reach. Without financial support, she still pressed on to see at least one life touched for the better. Her whole dreams were pro—people and people friendly, this little child born at a corner of the earth grew up to spark a fire that has today become a movement of change. Think about how many millions of people will forever be grateful for the day she was born. In my opinion, this is a true reflection of the character of leadership. How many people are you touching for good? How many faces are smiling because of you? You can start where you are now with the little you have. If our governments, societies and schools had more Mother Teresa's today the world would literally become heaven in no time. There is a high demand for character, people with integrity, honesty and passion. As you develop in leadership be sure to develop in the right direction because the next revolution could actually depend on you. Bonnie Tyler said:

> Where are all the good men gone
> And where are all the goods
> Where's the street wise Hercules to fight the rise in us, Isn't there a white knight upon the private seas
> Holding out for a hero.

Begin to look into your family, organisation or even country. There is something you were born to change. As you reach out to people, God will not leave you untouched, your own needs and cares will also be met. Remember the best way to go up is to help another get up. Don't just lead, lead to change.

CHAPTER TEN:

STREAMS OF LEADERSHIP

Leaders are agents of change, they create an atmosphere of possibility around them, and they tend to set the tone and pace in their areas of operation. They don't wait for things to happen, they make things happen. Leadership is a critical issue in the development of Third World countries. It should not be taken likely if we are going to experience change.

Being a leader yourself; these are important questions to answer honestly. There are various leadership styles, I call them streams of leadership, that carry along with them various levels of productivity and prosperity.

1) Leadership by Position
2) Leadership by Delegation
3) Leadership by Intimidation
4) Leadership by Manipulation
5) Leadership by Inspiration

No one is born a great leader, but everyone is born a potential leader

The position you occupy on the leadership ladder is very important. It determines how much change your leadership can produce.

1. Leadership By Position

My high school days were critical to my formation as a person. I appreciate immensely the growth that took place within these six years. Many things that were put into me then, still form the basis of my lifestyle today. I went to one of the two military high schools in my country, Nigeria. It was a boarding school. The name Air Force Military School was not for fun at all. We were taught how to shoot guns; we constantly dressed in military uniforms. The training was very tough for young boys in their teens. I remember trying to run away several times but to no avail. More than half of us who started didn't finish, few died, and some left. My father being formerly an Air Force personnel made sure I finished despite my continuous threat letters and pressure from my mother and sisters. Prior to this time, I was still physically lazy and fat but of course all this changed.

Leadership is too delicate to delegate just to anyone

I never saw myself as a leader at this point. I didn't know at the time that no one is born a great leader but everyone is born a potential leader. I never handled the responsibility of supervising and instructing. I was just a normal ordinary student. By the time we got to the third year of Junior School, it was time for the school to choose prefects usually called junior provosts who would oversee affairs in the Junior School section. Those who wanted to be appointed would usually start helping to run the Junior School section; they would ensure that all was in order. The aim was to show that you were responsible enough to be appointed a provost. It was called 'patching'. The tough and rough guys who were strong and bossy were usually chosen. This particular time however the school had a new commandant. He made several changes which included the best three in each class, being chosen as junior leaders; this was a shift from physical to mental strength. Wow!!! Many of those tough boys were disappointed. I, and others who fell into this category, were chosen. Most of us just had the brains but not the other characteristics; so I thought anyway. Some of us were too gentle to occupy such posts but what could we do? duty called us.

This was my first time handling a leadership position so to speak. I was leading close to one hundred students; a new terrain, a new experience. The position gave me time to learn and develop at an early age how to handle and relate to people. However, I noticed that some guys who were not provosts, those tough ones were even more dreaded than I. They seemed to be able to make things happen. Many times I had to threaten my mates with the school authorities if they didn't comply with my orders. Little did I know that the position was not enough? I had to express leadership traits to earn the respect the position could bring. Some respected me because of the position not my function. This form of leadership is a deceptive one. Do not be fooled by the position you occupy in that family or office, a position is simply an exalted hill that makes one visible to others. If it is given to you when you are not ready you will probably make a fool of yourself. I would rather advise you to look for where to function, so that when position comes as a reason of your development and function; it makes a better opportunity to demonstrate your leadership. There is no future in any job; the future is in the man. The man makes the job; the job doesn't make the man.

2. Leadership by Delegation

I am fully aware that I am not at the end of the road in my leadership development, but I sincerely appreciate the fact that I am not where I used to be. Something happened to me in senior high five that really started changing my perception about leadership. Even after my appointment as a junior school provost which lasted for a year, progressing into senior high never made much difference for me. I still felt I wasn't much of a leader.

Delegation is opportunity presented for promotion

The senior high six students were going for camp meeting. This meant that all senior prefects chose students from senior high five to lead in their place while they go for the camp meeting. It was left for the senior prefects to choose who they deemed fit; it was meant to last for three weeks. One's ability to inspire and control was considered, toughness and strength were physical abilities amongst others that were also considered. To my greatest surprise when the list was read out, I was called as the senior prefect of my squadron. I wondered what it was that had led to this. I had not 'patched', never even expected it. Today I know better. I never knew I was developing. The period I served as a junior prefect helped me grow almost unconsciously. Now I had hundreds of students under my control. This however was leadership by delegation. This is when you are given leadership responsibility to carry out by a higher authority within a time frame. It usually serves as a time test for you. It will determine whether you will be promoted or demoted. Your performance is strictly watched at this stage of leadership. At this point, you haven't earned the respect you demand. It is given because of the higher authority who gave you the responsibility.

This is however a stepping stone for those who use it well. Do you know any leader who is presently a leader by delegation? How well is he doing?

Delegation gives
- Borrowed Authority
- Borrowed Credibility
- Exposure and Experience
- Opportunity.

Develop your ability to motivate and communicate; then you will have no need to intimidate

During my three weeks as a delegated leader, I had all the authority and credibility of my superior. When I acted and talked. It was as though he were doing it in person. I later ended up becoming the senior prefect of my squadron.

It seemed there was an aura around me that just took me to the top wherever I went. When I got to university, I was given major leadership roles after just a year; a position no one had occupied in just one year of schooling. After three years, I started a personal development organisation which I was head over. The leader kept coming out. All the opportunities given me to lead, were all gradually contributing to my leadership development. Be smart enough to know that when a delegated opportunity comes your way, you should make the best of it: that might just be the door to the next level.

3. Leadership by Intimidation

This form of leadership is responsible for the state of many Third World countries today. It does not respect human law and human rights. It functions by the excessive use of force and power. This style of leadership has no respect for the character and expression of leadership. Followers are made to adhere to commands, whether the orders are moral or immoral.

These kind of leaders do not inspire or motivate. They are above the law. Hold on! before you start thinking of certain names. This could even apply to parents who don't communicate well with their children; no growing relationship and familiarity between both parties. It is all about what the parents want and not the children. This form of leadership thrives on threats; people are locked up unjustly, sacked from their jobs with no fair trial because they refuse to adhere to certain tyrants and dictators. This kind of leadership is negative. It is off the tangent of leadership values. Leaders with selfish ambitions, low self esteem and insecurity are the ones who normally adapt this style of leadership. It has never brought development and never will. Begin to build your ability to inspire, motivate and communicate and you will have no need to intimidate.

4. Leadership by Manipulation

Let's paint the scenario of an executive who is male and his female assistant. This female assistant is a very pretty and smart woman. She is also very ambitious and wants to be the best she can be, climbing the ladder of management in her career. Having a close working relationship with her boss, he is aware of all her ambitions. She works round the clock to distinguish herself among her co-workers.

To manipulate is to demonstrate a leader's inability to initiate and motivate.

Her boss who happens to be her mentor begins to try to get intimate with her even though he is married. He promises her many benefits such as trainings abroad, promotions, and juicy projects at work and so on if she would only accept his advances. He plays on her legitimate desires and tries to take advantage of her. This kind of leadership is selfish in nature, it takes advantage of the legitimate desires of followers and tries to get them to do things with promise to fulfill their desire. This kind of leadership is deceptive; it tends to use the desires of its followers as a bait to get them to do things, even wrong things. It is not a pure form of leadership and doesn't bring out the best in people.

If such a woman refuses her boss, you can imagine the pressure she will be under at work. Her productivity at home and work will certainly drop. If she decides to play along, the stability of the home of her boss is negatively affected. Any which way, there is a drop in productivity. The end of such leadership is distrust and disloyalty. In no time the followers too begin to be deceptive. This builds and creates an atmosphere that is not conducive to growth and productivity. Are you this kind of leader? I hope not. If you are, begin to change. If we can be patient to develop our leadership properly and take our cue from those who are role models, we will soon discover that there are better and more effective ways of getting things done.

Leaders who care for those they lead are followed by those they lead

5. Leadership by Inspiration

This is the highest and most effective form of leadership. This is leadership at its peak, leaders who lead by inspiration function by

- Vision
- Communication
- Demonstration
- Motivation . . .

At this level of leadership, followers gladly follow their leaders notwithstanding how tough the terrain might be. Followers are ready to die for the cause. This happens when they find a leader they can trust, one who has developed in character and models the leadership he professes. The man who cares for those he leads is loved by his followers. Such a leader cannot be hidden; he is like a speck of light giving direction in a dark world. There is no need for intimidation, manipulation or even coercion. The windows of history have all the facts, that leading by this method has the highest and greatest effect. You don't have to hold a position just possess an inspiring vision that is targeted at making people better and bigger. Continuously cast the vision, demonstrate it and watch your follower's exhibit mind-blowing service. This kind of leadership respects human law and dignity. It is the true atmosphere for productivity.

Another Inspiration

Nelson Rolihlahla Mandela was born on July 18th, 1918. He was the first President of South Africa to be elected in a fully representative democratic election. Before his Presidency, he was a prominent antiapartheid activist who, while imprisoned for 27 years, was involved in the planning of underground armed resistance activities. The struggle was, for Mandela, a last resort. He remained steadfast and committed to non-violence. Throughout his 27 year imprisonment, much of it spent in a cell on Robben Island, Mandela became the most widely known figure in the struggle against South African apartheid regime and nations sympathetic to it considered him and the ANC to be terrorists, the armed struggle was an integral part of the overall campaign against apartheid. The switch in policy to that of reconciliation, which Mandela pursued upon his release in 1990, facilitated a peaceful transition to a fully representative democracy in South Africa.

Leaders with the power of inspiration are able to enact elevation

Having received over a hundred awards over four decades, Mandela is currently a celebrated elder statesman who continues to voice his opinion on topical issues. In South Africa, he is known as Madiba, an honorary title adopted by elders of the Mandela clan. The title has come to be synonymous with Nelson Mandela. Many South Africans also refer to him reverently as 'inkhulu' (grandfather).

By now you should have been able to identify the stream you are flowing in, remember no one is born a great leader but 'everyone' is born a potential leader. We must begin to develop our leadership in the right direction. There is a need for true leaders; many parts of the earth are in a dilapidated state. The lives of many are at stake, families need to be raised, businesses need to be born, organisations need to be driven, countries need revolutions; wherever you are, brace up and make a difference, you are made differently for that very purpose.

CONCLUSION:

ACTION

GIANT TODDLER Such a
vast expanse Blessed but
bound Talented but
tortured Such a great
nation Severed by two
waters Knitted at the
centre Lubricated from
its shoe! Fluent in three
tongues Such a revered
nation Sending
ambassadors
To the ends of the earth
Such a beautiful people
Dark, coloured and goodly
Suffering amidst plenty
Suffering but smiling
Languishing but laughing
Such a beloved nation
A towering giant, so immerse
Yet still an accursed toddler
Saint Moses Eromosele

Does this describe your life and country or that of someone
you know? It is the description of many countries and that
is the reason for our crusade. At the time this book was

conceived, it could even describe my situation, there was so much inside me that was yet untapped. Many have been here and many have come out; that means you have hope. If you have not jumped to this page but have carefully gone through the wealth of information presented with attention, I congratulate you in advance for an anticipated explosion.

The state of your psychology will determine your propensity for prosperity

As you have fed your mind with thoughts, allow the thoughts to grip your mind. It is at this level your psychology changes. You have gone through the book allow the book go through you. Allow the thoughts to incubate your mind and heart leaving you pregnant. It will produce deep ideas, imaginations and visions in you; it will ignite you with passion, producing power for a better life. Incubate them, feed on them, and attend to them and in no time you will deliver them.

Every theology produces a psychology and every psychology produces a particular activity. The rightness of your psychology will increase your propensity for prosperity. I believe certain mental configurations that have not enhanced production have been replaced with more productive ways of thinking at this point. Don't stay attached to your old ways of doing things. Be humble and hungry enough for something better and something bigger, you will experience a transformation.

I must say at this point that information is not just for education, it is for application. Information is like a grenade, with the capacity to explode but when the pin is not removed it remains power in potential form. The ignition key is application. No matter what you have read and learnt, until information is mixed with application, production will never be the output. It will be painful to know you read this book without any positive change because that will be defeating the purpose for which this book was written. Congratulations once again. Having got past the hurdle of reading, now begin to apply. You are now that time bomb, unlock yourself by the force of application and watch yourself explode with productivity and prosperity in your world.

Information is not just for education but for application

This book would have been published long ago but the challenge of writing a book was scary. It made me passive. I couldn't just embrace responsibility and get myself to work. I knew it would change my life and the lives of many who read it. But I unconsciously folded my hands saying "Someday, sometime, I will write"; the point to deal with here is procrastination. No matter how lofty your ideas are, they are not enough. You must put the wheels to your dreams. Procrastination will steal the possibility of success today. It will keep pushing your day of delivery, giving you an imaginary and false sense of satisfaction. There is always a time to wake up from your dreams and get to work. A journey of a thousand miles begins with the first step. Fear is false evidence appearing real, face your fears, you can jump the hurdles and climb the mountains, you have more than what it takes to make it in life. Your situation is not damaged beyond repair; neither is that of your country. No matter how deep the locust and canker worms have eaten; with the application of tried and tested principles change is inevitable, success is sure. I made up my mind a long time ago, success or nothing else; I will not accept any substandard life. It looked far, it looked impossible, many thought I was too ambitious but today it is a different story altogether. We are only just beginning, the world is in view. Pick up your dreams, life is the proof of hope, you can have a better life you can have a better future if you will begin now.

As we begin to coast home, I would like to emphasise that every part of this book has its unique purpose in the

The ignition key for explosion, is application, turn it on.

accomplishment of the overall purpose. Some chapters might seem more interesting than others depending on your particular wiring, present area of need and your field of practice. I will however advise that to enjoy the full benefit that this book has the capacity to bring, you should have carefully gone through every page to get a full dose of the prescriptions I provide. Productivity and prosperity are all realities, brace up and face life; let me hear from you and all your exploits from now on. Let us team up together united in mind and spirit bringing change to our lives and the lives of many around us.

Many people, families, organisations and countries being the complicated systems that they are, will require several prescriptions from various angles of an economy to have a holistic effect. I have only presented prescriptions and solutions from my own area of expertise as a National Reformer. There are still more books to come. As this work is combined with others in other fields, Third World countries are bound to be trailblazers in no time. As powerful as this book may be I am careful not to overestimate its value, I do not in any terms doubt its role and relevance in our time and day but neither do I claim to have all the answers. It will however give you the needed thrust to create a better life for you and your environment.

With every take off, there is a landing, a final whistle to every football match, an end to every beginning. I would love to curtain with the first poem I ever wrote. It exposes my heart; it takes off my garments and reveals my passions. It expresses why I wrote this book and the many others to come, it is the very reason I breathe and live. As you read it I believe the same fire that drives me will catch up with you and together we can bring lasting and true change to the continent of Africa, other Third World countries and the human race. It is titled "The Answer".

The Answer

There is a cry from the Nile
Going beyond the mountains high Up above where
the eagles fly Soaring on the wings of the sky
To all who live in prophecy and destiny
To climb the ladder of productivity and prosperity
Giving a helping hand to humanity A cry for a
leader who is a healer A reader shaker and a
mover Dreaming believing and acting
One who knows the way so he can say
The what the why and the where
Unveiling the how that brings about the wow
Steps to terminate struggles
An initiator a Navigator
Seeing a need and taking the lead Taking heed in
the midst of every deed Accepting responsibility
for activity Who will hear this cry
From the depths of the earth The crest of the
mountains Who will hear this cry
For one who can be the sun as we run
Could it be a nun or is there none
A cry for a song in the midst of a storm
To soothe the wounded tooth
Rays of light even when things are tight
The wine to give a shine even when things don't
seem fine
Comfort to soothe challenges
Faith to dilute fear
Courage for conquest
Who will hear this cry
Who will bring us productivity and prosperity
Do you hear this same cry
It hovers over Nigeria roaring through Africa deep
into the Third World